Crisis, Disaster, and Risk

Crisis, Disaster, and Risk

Institutional Response and Emergence

Kyle Farmbry

Routledge
Taylor & Francis Group

LONDON AND NEW YORK

First published 2013 by M.E. Sharpe

Published 2015 by Routledge
2 Park Square, Milton Park, Abingdon, Oxon OX14 4RN
711 Third Avenue, New York, NY 10017, USA

Routledge is an imprint of the Taylor & Francis Group, an informa business

Library of Congress Cataloging-in-Publication Data

Farmbry, Kyle, 1970–
  Crisis, disaster, and risk : institutional response and emergence / by Kyle Farmbry.
    p. cm.
  Includes bibliographical references and index.
  ISBN 978-0-7656-2419-2 (hbk. : alk. paper)—ISBN 978-0-7656-2421-5 (pbk. : alk. paper)
1. Emergency management. 2. Disaster relief. 3. Risk–Sociological aspects. I. Title.

HV551.2.F37 2012
658.4'77—dc23   2012000156

ISBN 13: 9780765624215 (pbk)
ISBN 13: 9780765624192 (hbk)

Contents

Preface   vii

Introduction: Crisis, Disaster, and
    Risk in a Late-Modern Era   xi

Part I. Natural Disasters as Crises   1

  1. Optimism Interrogated: The Earthquakes and
     Tsunamis of 1755 and 2004   5
  2. Earthquakes and Progressive-Era Revival   19
  3. Limits of the Built Environment: Hurricanes and
     Choices of Locality   30

Part II. Global Public Health   47

  4. Plague as Crisis and Corollary to Societal Change   51
  5. Germ Theory, Cholera, and Infectious Disease   65
  6. Infectious Disease and Nascent Public Health
     Infrastructures: The 1918 Influenza Epidemic   73
  7. Twentieth-Century Optimism   84
  8. HIV/AIDS   98
  9. Anticipated Health Crises   108

Part III. Technology, Science, and Crisis   117

  10. The Multiple Crises of a Nuclear Era   120
  11. Balancing the Optimism and Risks of Civilian
      Nuclear Energy   133
  12. Hazardous Waste   143

13. Industrial Accidents and Determining Liability: Bhopal   151
14. Oil   158

Conclusion: Toward New Institutional Frameworks for
    Mitigating Risks and Potential Crises   170

Bibliography   179
Index   185
About the Author   195

Preface

No problem can be solved from the same consciousness that created it.
—Albert Einstein

We tend not to think about crises much—that is, until they happen. It is often then that we begin to ask ourselves a myriad of questions with the intention of further understanding the complex dynamics of the situation at hand. Why did this happen? What specific incidents are related to this? How did the various sequences of events develop? What are the roles of various responders? How are the survivors managing? What can we—individually, locally, regionally, nationally, or even internationally—do either to prevent this from happening again or to minimize the impact of such an event in the future?

I found myself asking questions similar to these in 2004. A few days after Christmas, I sat glued to the television set in my central Istanbul hotel. I was only a few hours off a plane from Beirut, where I had spent the previous week celebrating the marriage of one of my friends from college, Kamal. He and his new wife, Marianne, were now off celebrating their honeymoon on various beaches in Malaysia and Thailand. At my hotel bar, however, I found myself fearing the worst for them: Phuket, one of Kamal and Marianne's destinations, was suddenly all over the news as one of the sites where a tsunami of unprecedented magnitude had hit the shores on the morning of December 26, a few days before my having access to news of the events. Now recognized as one of the worst natural disasters of recent history, the tsunami resulted in over 250,000 deaths in the fourteen countries impacted. Thousands of others were left with major injuries, and still others were displaced for months, if not years, thereafter.

The next few days consisted of a flurry of e-mails and calls to other wedding guests. Had we heard from Kamal and Marianne? Did anyone know if they were okay? With each image of the impacted areas, and each interview with eyewitnesses and survivors, we found our dread rising as we feared the worst for our friends.

About a week after the tsunami hit Phuket, the e-mail arrived: "We are okay," Kamal wrote. The two of them had been on higher ground the morning of the tsunami—and were safe. While many of us breathed a sigh of relief at this news, thousands of others were not so fortunate. The days and weeks that followed brought numerous stories of communities that were affected by the crisis and many more stories of lives lost.

The tragedy of the Asian tsunami started what was to be a year of tremendous crises all over the world. The tsunami was followed a few months later by summer floods throughout Europe, Hurricane Katrina in September, and an earthquake in Kashmir in October. Ultimately, the combined tragedies within that twelve-month cycle led the World Health Organization to ask if 2005 was a year of natural disasters (Braine 2006, 4).

For me, the tsunami began a several-year journey of thinking about emergencies and crises. How do we conceptualize them? How do we absorb the individual stories of human tragedy with the magnitude of the statistics that frequently accompany wide-scale crisis? What types of responses can we develop? What are the roles of various societal institutional actors in responding to them? From the perspective of an academic—what theoretical and methodological frameworks are behind our conceptualization and response to crises? From the nonacademic and nonanalytical perspective of simply existing as another being in the same world, where tragedy begets loss—what are the proper means for demonstrating a sense of caring and concern?

I tend to look at 2005 not so much as a year of disasters, but rather as a year in which there was a shift in how we thought about disasters, at least in the short term. Questions of place and proximity, community resilience, and the human spirit all surfaced in much of the discourse related to disaster during this period. The images of children who lost parents in the tsunami led us to give of our personal and financial resources in unprecedented amounts globally, and the stories of people who lost their homes as a result of Hurricane Katrina encouraged many of us to open our communities to them.

Crisis, Disaster, and Risk: Institutional Response and Emergence is the result of my reflection and sense-making on crises between 2005 and 2011. The book emerges from the recognition that an increasing number of emergencies, of varying forms and magnitudes, have surfaced in recent years and my contention that agencies need to adapt their patterns of response based on lessons learned from each new crisis. It also stems from my belief that we need to start thinking about crises and disasters not only from a framework of incident reporting, but also from a framework that encourages reflection on connectivity and complexity. By adopting a framework that attempts to incorporate questions of theory and historical connectivity, I both hope and anticipate that we will identify ways to reduce the tolls of the next disaster.

Oddly, the final months of my completion of this book coincided with the emergence of several disasters, which forced me to think further about how we conceptualize such events. In January 2010, as I was finishing the first draft of a chapter on earthquakes, Haiti and then Chile were struck by major earthquakes. In April, the Eyjafjallajökull volcano in Iceland erupted, disrupting air travel around the world. The explosion of the *Deepwater Horizon* rig and the resulting oil spill off the Louisiana coast in April 2010, now recognized as the worst oil spill in U.S. history, caused major reflection on responses to disasters. Finally, the earthquake, tsunami, and nuclear crisis in Japan in March 2011 provided a basis for asking questions about the intersection between crises that had both technological and natural causes as critical underpinnings. With each crisis, I came to recognize that another would be inevitable. I also came to recognize the value of any conversation on how we collectively build systems for mitigating, as best we can, the human toll after such crises and disasters.

The final months of my working on *Crisis, Disaster, and Risk* reaffirmed for me that like most endeavors worth undertaking, the writing of a book is something that does not occur in isolation. This book is no different. Stages of the walk on this journey were accompanied by people who provided encouragement that, in hindsight, was truly far more than one could have requested. In particular, I want to thank Deidre and Larry Farmbry, Mike and Heather Libonatti, Steve Levy, Daryl Nann, Anne Visser, Steve Lanier, Kamal and Marianne Siblini, and Christina Cantrill.

Current and former students, including Cheryl Gaffney, Seth Mann, Jongmin Shon, Sontaia Briggs, Alex Henderson, Jyldyz Kasymova, Al Passarella, Caitlin Scuderi, Carissa Meyer, Portia Dinoso, Jenn Mendoza, Azeem Chaudry, Laura Chinchilla, Ashley Whitaker, Christine Awe, Gizelle Clemens, Stefani Krol, Mateus Baptista, Rachel Niemczyk, and Mariana Giordano, provided research support at various points in this book's development. Michael Vorgetts served as a critical right hand for much of this project by helping to coordinate much of the research process and many of the early teams of graduate student researchers. Sharon Stroye, Mahako Etta, and Dorothy Knauer helped to ensure that I was able to have the time to focus on this book by assisting me in reaching other deadlines and completing other tasks. Marissa Beach, Hawwa Huhammad, Katherine Krick, and Lourdes Alers provided research assistance in the latter stages of the book's development. Christen Madrazo provided rounds of editorial and content feedback.

Finally, in writing this book, I came across numerous stories of people who volunteered, risked their safety, and confronted the challenges and realities that come with disasters and crises. This effort of mine pales in comparison to what they have done or will do in the context of saving lives and rebuilding communities. Although I have met only a few of them and have read only a handful of their stories, I think it appropriate that I, and the author of any book on crisis and disaster issues, keep their sacrifices at the forefront while thinking about documenting and reflecting on experiences and situations that they have literally faced. This book is in dedication to them and in appreciation for the sacrifices that they have made.

Ultimately, I hope our overall considerations of crises encountered and those yet to be encountered might provide a context for thinking a bit differently as we confront new ones and prepare for those that we are certain to face in the future. This book is my attempt to affect, even marginally, the way we shape this discourse.

Introduction

Crisis, Disaster, and Risk
in a Late-Modern Era

On the morning of January 17, 1995, much of the city of Kobe, Japan, found itself under rubble as a result of what became known as the Great Hanshin Earthquake. The suddenness of the crisis caught many people, including political and civic leaders, off guard. What ultimately transpired between the three hundred fires that erupted and the six thousand deaths that directly or indirectly resulted from the quake were a number of questions about the social, economic, and political forces related to disasters. In time, Kobe's experiences served as the impetus for shaping earthquake-response activity in Japan, as well as for thinking internationally about crisis and emergency issues. Japan had experienced quakes before, and it most certainly would experience them again. The Kobe quake, however, provided a point of reflection on a number of critical questions about how government and civil society actors respond to a major crisis.

Ten years later, on December 26, 2004, the world experienced what became one of the deadliest natural disasters in recent memory when an earthquake struck under the sea near Indonesia, releasing a deadly tsunami that would strike several nations and result in the deaths of over 250,000 people and the displacement of an additional two million others. The tsunami engendered an enormous response from individuals and agencies around the globe. The International Red Cross and Red Crescent launched the largest relief and response effort in their histories, and hundreds of other nongovernmental organizations engaged in efforts to respond to the tsunami. The efforts of these agencies, coupled with those of governmental and intergovernmental actors such as the United Nations, the World Health Organization, and the World Bank, leveraged a major conversation on disaster response. Central to this conversation were three thematic questions. First, how should institutions at the local, national, and international levels respond to each disaster? Second, what was the human role in shaping the causal factors related to the disaster? Third, what lessons could be learned from each disaster to lessen the destructive impact of the future crises we would encounter?

Recent decades have provided opportunities for people working in governments and students of government to reflect actively on matters of disaster and crisis. We have witnessed the natural crises of the tsunami of 2004 and of Katrina less than a year later. We have experienced crises in health arenas, wrestling, for example, with the growing toll from HIV/AIDS and the suddenness of SARS or the appearance of the avian flu. Technology and industrial advancement have been linked to a wide range of crises. Nuclear incidents, such as those at Three Mile Island, Chernobyl, and most recently the Fukushima Daiichi nuclear complex, have enabled us to ponder technology's limits and possible costs in our quest for additional sources of energy. Environmental crises such as the Deepwater Horizon oil spill have enabled us to reflect on the wisdom of going beyond where we can reach unaided with complex machinery in our attempt to obtain oil.

FRAMING DISASTER AND CRISIS: A HISTORICAL CONTEXT

"After I had drawn myself together I found my way to my home, where, thank God, the wreck had not been as complete as many others I had witnessed," noted Fred Hewitt, one of the survivors of the 1906 San Francisco earthquake. "Then it was that I realized the condition of an excitement-crazed populace." His observation continued:

> Herds of huddled creatures, attired in next to nothing, occupied the center of the streets, not knowing what would happen next or which way they should turn for safety. Each and every person I saw was temporarily insane. Laughing idiots commented on the fun they were

having. Terror marked their faces, and yet their voices indicated a certain enjoyment that maniacs have when they kill and gloat over their prey. Women, hysterical to an extreme point, cried and raved for those they loved when they were standing at their elbow. Mothers searched madly for their children who had strayed, while little ones wailed for their protectors. (Hewitt 1906)

Hewitt's observations, along with those of many of the other survivors of the quake, helped to embed the 1906 San Francisco earthquake in our collective consciousness as the disaster against which we measured future earthquakes in the United States. With shocks felt from Oregon to the south of Los Angeles, the earthquake ultimately impacted thinking and development of initial administrative frameworks for conceptualizing disasters. It also helped to frame a number of questions about who should respond to them—should government agencies be the primary respondent, or is it the role of other actors?

Eleven years following the San Francisco quake, on December 6, 1917, a munitions explosion in Halifax, Canada, resulted in the deaths of over 2,000 people and injuries to an additional 9,000 people. This disaster provided the impetus for what is recognized as the foundational piece of disaster research: S.H. Prince's 1920 study *Catastrophe and Social Change*, which ultimately served as one of the models against which later disaster studies were compared.

Catastrophe and Social Change used a sociological framework for shaping explorations of disasters. Prince focused on how individuals and groups reacted to the explosion and how such reactions could be used to enhance our understanding of what might be "predictable social movements" that stem from large-scale emergencies. His depiction of the disaster was presented during a critical era when sociology, political science, economics, and other areas of the social sciences were in the process of being galvanized as distinct academic fields and, in many cases, were providing forums for exploring how various elements of modern industrial life—including the tragic ones such as crises or disasters—would be examined.

San Francisco and Halifax occurred in the midst of a period of reflection on the process of developing relief strategies for communities that had recently confronted crises. Underscoring both disasters were questions of which institutions should be involved with relief and recovery efforts. Was there a specific role for government? Were there voluntary efforts that might be the most apt for providing relief and recovery? These questions helped to shape an emergent discourse, intersecting various disciplines with broader issues of the roles of governmental and ultimately nongovernmental actors in responding to risks or crises.

In the midst of the Great Depression, after years of debate on the role of government in disaster relief, Congress passed the 1936 Flood Control Act. This act designated the first extensive involvement of the federal government in flood relief. Aside from the significance of the government's formal role in direct flood relief, the passage of the act signified several important patterns within American society. First, it represented a resource and role shift. For the first time in the nation's history, the federal government was able to leverage the capital and human resources to make flood abatement a reality. Federal officials also demonstrated a vision of a federal government role in flood relief. A significant number of political and administrative decision makers increasingly saw a role for government in responding to the crises that their populations faced and would face in the future. This shift occurred as part of the change in perspective that was marking the government's role within the emergent concept of a welfare state at the time. Government was recognizing that much of its role consisted in providing for the needs of its more vulnerable members—and disasters provided clear examples of when such vulnerability might surface.

The passage of the Flood Control Act also demonstrated the growing realization of the impact of population changes. Because there were more people living in urban areas by the 1930s, and because many of these areas were in potential flood zones, one of the questions related to flood relief involved the protection of these growing urban populations. How should government change its patterns of emergency response when geographic proximity places people close to one another and close to areas of potential disaster? Is the danger that people confront as a result of disaster ultimately due to the choices they make in terms of where they choose to situate themselves—and if so, what responsibility does the broader society have in light of such decisions? These questions of geography and situated space are at a critical center of many of our present conversations related to crises and disasters.

Much of the formal field of disaster studies arose in the years immediately following the end of World War II. In Europe and Japan, the field was driven by postwar rebuilding needs. In the United States, many of the studies were driven by cold war–era concerns about how communities in the United States would respond to disasters caused by a nuclear attack. In the 1950s and 1960s, the National Academy of Sciences and the National Research Council launched committees on disaster studies and supported a behavioral approach to explorations of disaster response.

The federal government provided additional support behind the growing field of disaster studies with the passing of the Disaster Relief Act of 1950. This act helped to coordinate relief studies and efforts and shaped what became the first coordinated alignment of federal resources for disasters and crisis management. During this era, the federal government also became involved with activities that encouraged risk taking in areas that could have had catastrophic results for populations. Specifically, federal encouragement of civilian use of nuclear power and involvement in the promotion of the use of new chemicals facilitated the increased use of various toxins that would lead to greater awareness of environmental risks.

Throughout the 1960s and early 1970s, several natural disasters led to the need for intervention at a federal level. Hurricanes Donna, Carla, Betsy, and Camille struck the United States between the years of 1960 and 1969. These hurricanes, coupled with the 1964 Alaskan earthquake, the San Fernando earthquake of 1971, and other smaller natural disasters, renewed questions about the appropriate role of federal government intervention in crises or emergencies. Some cases, specifically those of the four major hurricanes of the 1960s, gave rise to additional questions about human choice and locality. Was the scale of damage to human life and property due to Donna, Betsy, Carla, and Camille so great because of people's decisions to move to areas prone to hurricanes? If so, should government intervene in developing response, since choice by those in harm's way to move to more hurricane-prone areas played a role in the devastation they ultimately experienced?

In the 1970s, we witnessed the founding of numerous institutions to help us better understand and respond to disasters. Domestically, the nation's first assessment of research on natural hazards began at the Institute of Behavioral Sciences at the University of Colorado at Boulder in 1972. Internationally, the founding of the Center for Research on the Epidemiology of Disasters (CRED) in 1973 led to the development of an international research infrastructure for monitoring disasters and crises. Since then, CRED has been able to build a database of ongoing research related to disasters as well as to become a World Health Organization global program for emergency preparedness. In time, particularly with the advent of newer systems and processes for tracking characteristics of specific disasters, similar data management tools have enabled us to consider the complexities of various crises at a more detailed level than we previously could, as well as to draw lessons from which to compare strategies and response patterns in relation to crises that we may encounter.

In 1975, geographer Gilbert White and sociologist J. Eugene Haas published *Assessment of Research on Natural Hazards*, which drew largely upon work conducted at the University of Colorado in the Natural Hazards Research and Applications Information Center. The book served as an analysis of the nation's awareness of natural hazards and disasters during the 1970s. In their work, White and Haas observed that research on natural disasters had been dominated by physical scientists and engineers; they argued that little attempt had been made to better understand the economic, social, and political ramifications of such disasters. Through their examination of these approaches, they contended that by taking such social science perspectives into account, the nation could better understand both the causes of, and the potential reactions to, crises and disasters.

The late 1970s and 1980s witnessed their own share of crises that affected the overall discourse on disasters and crisis management. In 1979, the near meltdown of the nuclear reactor core at Three Mile Island brought to light the challenges of the technological, as opposed to natural, side of disasters. In the same year, the new awareness of the chemical waste at Love Canal in New York raised questions about how to respond to the ever-growing dangers of industrial waste. The 1984 Union Carbide disaster in India, taking the lives of over 3,000 people, raised the question of the impact of our industrial advancement on the well-being of human life. These incidents begat questions about the how late-industrial–era or late-modern realities related to crises and disasters. Two years after the Union Carbide disaster, the melt-down of the nuclear reactor at Chernobyl, in the then Soviet Union, again raised the specter of the potential emergencies related to nuclear power.

The last decade of the twentieth century brought about several transitions in the way we think about disasters. In 1992, Hurricane Andrew caused us to reflect on the role of the building and insur-ance industries in securing people prior to and following crises. Hurricane Andrew occurred after a several-year lull in major hurricanes to strike Florida and after years of both the migration of thousands of residents to hurricane-prone regions and the weakening of building codes in such regions. In Japan, the Kobe earthquake in 1995 brought global attention to the question of earthquakes and modern life, with an emphasis on the recognition of the existence of communities that are particularly vulnerable to crises. The Kobe earthquake was the first major disaster of the Internet era, thus marking the first time people around the world were able to receive updates on the response and recovery ef-forts in almost real time.

The 1990s also witnessed discussions on emergent threats in the area of infectious disease from a crisis framework. Driven largely by discourse surrounding the impact that HIV/AIDS had on nations since its emergence in the early 1980s, as well as the concerns related to the appearance of new threats such as Ebola and the avian flu, public health officials began to work with other government officials to identify ways to stem the potential threats of such crises. By the end of the decade, such concerns were reaching policy makers at the highest levels of national govern-ments and world bodies. In July 2000, for example, the United Nations Security Council debated the crisis of HIV/AIDS as one of the major threats of the present era. This discussion ultimately led the Security Council to adopt Resolution 1308, which placed HIV/AIDS within the UN's rubric of threats to international security.

The initial decade of the twenty-first century witnessed its own challenges related to crisis and disasters. Clearly, September 11, 2001, brought with it a domestic shift in the conceptualization of disaster as well as a response on both the domestic and international level. The passage of the Homeland Security Act shortly thereafter and the institutionalization of the Department of Homeland Security further galvanized a federal framework for preventing and responding to disasters as they might surface, this time, however, with an emphasis upon those disasters classified as terrorist acts.

In the middle of the decade, the tsunami of 2004 brought about numerous questions regarding the coordination of disaster relief in the face of wide-scale human tragedy. The tsunami occurred a few weeks prior to what was to have been a United Nations meeting on crisis and disaster issues known as the World Conference on Disaster Reduction, an event scheduled to coincide with the tenth anniversary of the 1995 earthquake in Kobe, Japan. The tragedy of the tsunami enabled the United Nations and other multinational agencies to frame the meeting, which was ultimately held in January 2005 in Kobe, to develop a ten-year plan devised to make the world safer from natural hazards. Known as the Hyogo Framework for Action, the plan consisted of a global blueprint for disaster-risk reduction efforts during the next decade.

The close of the decade brought both the 2010 earthquakes in Haiti and Chile and the BP oil spill in the Gulf of Mexico. Haiti and Chile provided a foundation for questions on the intersection of poverty and disaster response. How, we wondered, in looking at the devastation in both nations from earthquakes of roughly the same magnitude, could the severity of the destruction differ as much as it did between both nations? With the BP spill, we found ourselves questioning our combined wisdom in assuming the risk of drilling for oil in areas too deep to easily fix errors should they arise. Finally, in the first few months of the second decade of the new century, we witnessed the potential linkages between natural and technological crisis with the chain reaction of the earthquake, tsunami, and nuclear crisis that occurred in northern Japan and led to the disbursement of radioactive particles across the world's northern hemisphere.

LATE-MODERN FRAMEWORKS FOR CRISIS AND DISASTERS

In the early 1980s, James Short, then president of the American Sociological Association, called for a sociological framework for conceptualizing risk and disaster preparation. His focus was based largely on a criticism of risk analyses as they appeared in research. As he noted, "the focus of risk analysis on human life and health, and on economic values, has been too narrow" (Short 1984, 711).

Short's call to action coincided with reflections from other sociologists and social theorists exploring new strategies for conceptualizing risks and crises. Perrow (1984), for example, examined catastrophes that were related to high-risk fields. His normal accident theory, which evolved largely out of his experiences examining the Three Mile Island crisis in the late 1970s, provided a basis for conceptualizing the various interplays between advanced technology and human error that frequently are at the base of an increasing number of crises.

In the ten years following Short's challenge to his field, some scholars placed some of the risks that broader society faced in the context of the discourse on modernity and postmodernity that was occurring in the latter decades of the twentieth century. Critical to framing the components of this discourse were Anthony Giddens (1991, 1994) and Ulrich Beck (1992, 1994). Both Giddens and Beck wrestled with a notion of late modernity, which they proposed as an alternative to many of the theories of postmodernity being discussed at the time. As Giddens describes the late-modern world:

> [It] is apocalyptic, not because it is inevitably heading toward calamity, but because it introduces risks which previous generations have not had to face. However much there is progress towards international negotiation and control of armaments, so long as nuclear weapons

remain, or even the knowledge necessary to build them, and so long as science and technology continue to be involved with the creation of novel weaponry, the risk of massively destructive warfare will persist. Now that nature, as a phenomenon external to social life, has in a certain sense come to an "end"—as a result of its domination by human beings—the risks of ecological catastrophe form an inevitable part of our horizon of day-to-day life. Other high-consequence risks, such as the collapse of global economic mechanisms, or the rise of totalitarian superstates, are an equally unavoidable part of our contemporary experience. (Giddens 1991, 4)

According to Beck (1992), the interlinked processes of globalization, individualization, gender revolution, underemployment, and global risks have helped in the transition between stages of modernity and have left us with the challenge of reflecting on institutional roles within the context of such transitions. How, as the nature of risk changes in such an era, will institutions respond? What types of new institutions will emerge? How will these institutions respond to the challenges of the era, which, if the challenges of recent years are any indication, will be very different from the challenges we have encountered thus far?

Beck (1994) argues that global society has progressed beyond stages of premodernity and "simple" modernity, to an era that he refers to as one of "reflexive modernity." According to him, the era of simple modernity was characterized largely by the development of various industrial advances that facilitated the distribution of goods. In the case of the reflexive modern society, one that he also refers to as the "risk society," much of the characterization is based on the distribution of societal risks or dangers.

For Beck, addressing the challenges of this risk society requires the implementation of reflexive learning processes within institutions that balance out the realities of technological advancements with the potential costs to broader societies. This process of reflexive learning entails recognizing that there are several positions from which expertise surrounding a given situation might be demonstrated. No longer is expertise merely a result of scientific positioning—as a technical approach to expertise would entail—but rather, expertise or authority that might come from a diversity of perspectives—some of which may have been traditionally underrepresented in policy discourse on societal challenges. Ultimately, Beck suggests that integral to his proposed notion of a risk society is society's ability and willingness to reflect on the dilemmas through the lens of varied positions of expertise (traditional and nontraditional perspectives), as well as to consider the risks that surface with stages of technological and industrial advancement and to comprehend the costs of modernization.

As we reflect on the challenges posed by the various crises and emergencies we have confronted in recent decades, and as we ponder the inevitable ones to come, we find ourselves wrestling with a number of institutional questions related to disasters and emergencies. When should institutions become involved in disaster or emergencies? Would it be best at the preventive, response, relief, or recovery stage? How should institutions become involved? And, *which* institutions should become involved? These questions help to frame the discourse related to shaping how agencies respond to specific crises.

Ultimately, as we consider the realities of these risks and dangers that we face and will continue to face, we need to reflect on strategies for building the various creative solutions that will ultimately enable us to address the challenges of those future disasters and crises both identified and yet to be identified. This is where the imagination element comes into the broader discourse; our creativity in forecasting and developing potential solutions will be a critical element of our framing current and potential future responses to crises—be they natural, public-health related, or technological.

AN APPROACH TO EXPLORING DISASTERS, CRISES, AND RISKS

A few months before the September 11 attacks, a team of forecasters in the Federal Emergency Management Agency developed predictions of three disaster scenarios viewed as both highly probable and particularly worrisome. These scenarios included a terrorist attack in New York, a hurricane flooding New Orleans, and a major earthquake on California's San Andreas fault (Jaffe 2005). While to date, the third has not occurred, geologists and seismologists watching the fault believe it may only be a matter of time. The question is how, given our lessons of previous disasters, will we plan for and ultimately mitigate any potential impact or plan for the possibility of any crisis, such as this third predicted by FEMA forecasters or any others that we may confront in the future?

I have chosen to frame much of my exploration in *Crisis, Disaster, and Risk* with the attempt to interweave premodern, modern, and late-modern influences on the exploration of crises. In my considerations of crises and disasters through a historical lens, I have attempted to incorporate issues such as technological consideration, immediacy, and institutional roles in order to merge lessons learned in the premodern and modern eras with those of the late-modern. The shift from the premodern to the modern is the first critical transition that frames this exploration. It was this shift that helped to frame concepts of control or determinism that humankind felt regarding their environments and that ultimately set up divides between man and nature that influenced how crises were handled.

A central condition in recognizing the interplay between premodern, modern, and late-modern risk and disaster consideration is the notion that history matters. While I do believe there is quite a bit of value in comprehending various crises as they occur—with an emphasis on gathering as much current data as possible on crises at the moment—there is value in understanding the historical context to various crises. Thus, most of the chapters in *Crisis, Disaster, and Risk* incorporate historical as well as current frameworks for assisting readers in understanding some of the broader complexities related to the crises.

A second critical condition is the recognition that institutions matter. Institutions working in late-modern realities must develop new processes for conceptualizing risk. Whereas risk in a traditional modern era suggests the ability to forecast and control the future consequences of human action, risk in an era of late modernity suggests that the consequences of such human action are less predictable and less controllable. New risks cannot be isolated within a set of geographical and national boundaries, and thus the ability to engage in prevention, recovery, and response must be shared by institutional actors, often spanning across national boundaries.

One strategy for enhancing responses of institutional actors across boundaries is to reform institutions so that they incorporate a degree of self-awareness at the institutional level—a concept Beck (1994) refers to as "reflexivity." A reflexive organization is one that enables a degree of critical thought by internal stakeholders as well as by individuals who are engaged in the integration of the processes of late-modern systems. A reflexive organization is aware of the challenges and the various risks encountered and has devised a number of approaches to effectively address such risks.

With the attempt to address some of the challenges of disasters, crises, and risks in the late-modern era came the emergence and reformation of numerous institutions in recent decades. Many of these institutions were framed in the middle of the twentieth century, particularly as the true scale of various challenges of a modern, industrialized world were becoming increasingly evident. Global institutions such as the United Nations and the World Health Organization were developed to help manage some of the challenges and crises of the modern era. Critical considerations include whether these institutions will adapt, and how they will adapt, to late-modern realities as they attempt to balance various crises encountered today with those that will surface in the future.

ORGANIZATION OF THE BOOK

Crisis, Disaster, and Risk: Institutional Response and Emergence aims to provide a framework for the conceptualization of crisis and disaster for students in public administration, public affairs, and related disciplines. It assumes two major contextual factors about the environment that the current student and future practitioner of political and administrative processes will encounter. The first contextual factor is a belief that the future environment will have more crises and disasters than the policy actor of the past has confronted. Our challenges will arise in an environment of intense turbulence, and part of our task will be to identify ways to deal with such different forms of challenge. Underscoring some of the increased complexity is awareness that our interconnected knowledge about these dilemmas is greater than we have experienced.

The second contextual factor assumed by this book is that the environments in which administrative and political leaders are acting are far more internationally and globally connected than decision makers have encountered in the past. Thus, thinking about crises and disasters must take into account some of the globally interconnected dimensions related to their activities. A crisis in one part of the world is connected to crises all over the world. This interconnectivity and lack of geographic boundaries mirrors much of the broad sociological reality that Beck and Giddens describe.

The book is divided into three parts. Each explores cases of disaster by specific type. Part I examines natural disasters as crises. Examples include earthquakes, tsunamis, hurricanes, and some of the systems that have emerged through which we now better understand these phenomena. This section explores one of the pressing questions that have surfaced in recent studies and literature pertaining to crisis: how might the risk factors related to natural disasters be conceptualized? For example, knowing that the rapid changes in the geographic factors facing the earth are constant, we now realize that there are hundreds of earthquakes in any given year. The impact of such realizations on where people choose to locate themselves (in a region that is susceptible to earthquakes, for example) affects some of the political and administrative responses when an earthquake strikes.

Part II explores crises in the area of global public health. It examines six cases drawing from the premodern era and stretching to the late-modern. I begin with a study of the European plague cycles lasting from the 1400s to the 1700s. The plagues that occurred during this period played a critical role in setting in motion processes and societal changes that would ultimately shape broader systems. I continue with an examination of the emergence of germ theory and early epidemiological explorations of the spread of disease, with an emphasis on the spread of cholera in the mid-1800s. The study of cholera and questions of germ theory lead me to consider the flu of 1918—a global pandemic that ultimately took over twenty million lives. Next, I turn to the modern era of medical advancement, particularly in an era of assumed victories over polio, smallpox, malaria, and other dangers encountered. Next, I explore the issue of HIV/AIDS, its emergence, and some of the political debates and institutional evolution related to it. I conclude with an examination of health crises to come, drawing upon our recent global experiences with severe acute respiratory syndrome (SARS). I examine how each of these incidents injected a critical theme into public health discussions on the risk of enhanced viral infections as related to species leaps and enhanced transportation between groups of people.

Part III looks at the role of technology and science in crisis. I begin with a two-chapter examination of the crises of nuclear risks. The first of the chapters reviews such risks in a military context. The second studies them in a civilian context. Next, I explore the crisis and disaster that might come from issues of industrial pollutants and the recognized need to better ameliorate toxic wastes, drawing from the crisis of the Love Canal disaster of the late 1970s. Third, I explore risk as related to industrial accidents, drawing largely from the lessons of the Bhopal tragedy of the mid-1980s. I conclude the section with an examination of risks caused by oil spills with an emphasis on lessons from the Deepwater Horizon oil spill in 2010.

The final chapter in the book revisits questions related to institutional responses to crises, with a particular emphasis on those crises that emerge in a global society and are deeply grounded in the late-modern realities that Beck suggests. It is in this final chapter that I frame a link between the exploration of the crises examined throughout the book and institutional reflexivity.

Crisis, Disaster, and Risk

Part I

Natural Disasters as Crisis

Common belief would have it that nothing about Chicago's geography links it to earthquakes. However, the tremors that shook the city on the morning of April 18, 2008, proved that earthquakes can strike in unexpected places. As stories of the quake's impact began to circulate, people heard of the mild shaking of towers in downtown Chicago and much heavier trembling in some of the nearby towns. Calls poured into fire departments with reports of the tremor. People in several of the city's high-rises shared stories of the swaying of buildings and of being awakened by the jolts that occurred at about a quarter to five that morning.

This was not the first time that Chicago had been stricken by a quake. Nearly two hundred years earlier, between December 16, 1811, and February 7, 1812, Chicago and much of the Midwest felt a series of violent tremors that stemmed from under New Madrid, Missouri, a small town about 167 miles from St. Louis and known to be sitting at the center of thousands of fault lines that stretch across nearly a quarter of a million square miles of territory throughout the central United States. The tremor sequence in 1811 and 1812, which is now referred to as the New Madrid Sequence, was felt as far away as Toronto, Montreal, New Orleans, and South Carolina. Eliza Brian, a witness to the sequence, noted:

> On the 16th of December, 1811, about two o'clock, A.M. we were visited by a violent shock of an earthquake, accompanied by a very awful noise resembling loud but distant thunder, but more hoarse and vibrating, which was followed in a few minutes by the complete saturation of the atmosphere, with sulfurous vapor, causing total darkness. The screams of the affrighted inhabitants running to and fro, not knowing where to go, or what to do—the cries of the fowls and beasts of every species—the cracking of trees falling, and the roaring of the Mississippi—the current of which was retrograde for a few

minutes, owing, it is supposed to an irruption in its bed—formed a scene truly horrible. From that time, until about sunrise, a number of lighter shocks occurred; at which time one still more violent than the first took place, with the same accompaniments as the first, and the terror which had been excited in every one, and indeed in all animal nature, was now, if possible, doubled. (Dow 1849, 155)

Geological estimates place the number of earthquakes linked to the 1812 New Madrid quake sequence in the tens of thousands. Most of these were small and detectable by only the most sensitive instruments. Geologists also now estimate that the New Madrid fault lines experience major earthquakes every three to four hundred years. This cycle is a point of concern for experts who follow earthquakes closely, as these estimates would place the regions impacted by the New Madrid fault lines due for another major earthquake sometime near the end of the twenty-first century.

Current population densities of the major areas where the New Madrid fault lines reach and the areas where the quakes of 1811 were felt provide a basis of concern for risk assessors engaged with predicting future quake possibilities. With a current population of almost three million people, Chicago for example would face enormous consequences if it were to find itself confronted today by an earthquake on the scale of New Madrid. New Orleans or Montreal, with populations of more than 250,000 and 1.6 million respectively, would not fare much better.

Understanding both what happened as a result of the New Madrid sequence in the 1800s and the implications for today's seismological considerations is a small part of the conversation on earthquakes and the broader questions surrounding them. Underscoring each of our incidents with an earthquake is a critical bit of science related to much of the quake's cause. Fault lines, continental drift, and the frailty of the earth's crust provide much of the geological story underpinning the damage caused by earthquakes. However, critical questions related to the built environment, as well as the quality of structures, factor into discussions. Weakly built structures in areas of high seismic activity will often lead to dangerous situations for people in the structures. Large numbers of these structures, situated in rapidly growing cities, will lead to greater risks of harm for greater numbers of people.

The chapters in this section explore cases of natural disaster many of which raise a critical question of whether there is indeed such a thing as a natural disaster. Factors of human choice provide a critical role in the selection of locations, the economic factors, and some of the political issues that underscore some of the disasters we have come to acknowledge.

I begin with a comparative examination of tsunamis. My comparison assumes a historical framework, as I examine the Lisbon tsunami of 1755 and the 2004 Indian Ocean tsunami. With both disasters, I review conceptualizations of optimism and human control to further establish themes that surface in other crises examined throughout the book. In Lisbon, optimism became a critical means by which people made sense of a disaster or crisis. For some people, incidents such as the tsunami of 1755 were perceived as merely a manifestation of God's will, regardless of the loss caused. Others used the incident to begin to critically reflect on humankind's role in shaping our own destinies. As a result of the second response, more critically inquisitive people began to explore questions, both in the context of the Lisbon tsunami and in the case of other disasters or crises experienced, that allowed for rapid scientific and medical advances that helped launch people on paths toward a modern state. In 2004, optimism of late modernity, which was driven largely through an appreciation of our advances in science, enabled people to find themselves lulled into a state of believing that we could predict or control various disasters. Unexpected crises such as the tsunami that struck nations surrounding the Indian Ocean in December of that year forced us to rethink how we conceptualized our abilities of prediction and control.

I continue with an examination of earthquakes and the societal changes that have stemmed from them. Before a crisis such as an earthquake, life exists in a certain way. Then, a sudden change occurs in the form of a major seismic happening, and life as it was known is forever altered. However, behind the incidents of various earthquakes are matters of human choice. In the aftermath of one of the central quakes examined—the 1906 San Francisco earthquake—vital decisions were made regarding how to rebuild the city and how to present the decisions to rebuild.

I conclude this section with an examination of hurricanes, intertwined with the choices people make to live in certain regions that are more vulnerable to such events. I begin the chapter with an examination of the 1900 hurricane in Galveston, Texas, where one of the worst hurricanes in U.S. history flooded the city and took the lives of over six thousand of its residents. To this day, the Galveston hurricane retains the position of being the disaster that is responsible for claiming the most lives in U.S. history. Galveston brought about a number of questions related to disaster and geography. The city was situated on an island at sea level in a zone where hurricanes had been known to strike. Yet people continued to move there. Galveston also brought up questions related to rebuilding after a disaster. Clear policy choices were made by city officials to alter the built environment of the city— to the extent of raising land and building seawalls as means of protection measures against future hurricanes.

In the decades following Galveston, there were numerous questions related to whether or not we could effectively plan for and, to a degree, control the various elements that confronted our cities and towns. We would over the years encounter hurricanes of various scales of intensity, whose destructiveness often was the result of both hurricane force and the evolution of years of public policy that impacted the decisions people made about where to live. I end with 2005's Hurricane Katrina, an event that served as a catalyst in framing discussions not only on a crisis, but also on the deeper dynamics of historical legacy, environmental complexity, and economic disparity in a region susceptible to disaster.

Ultimately, my goal in this section is to explore the interaction between risk and disasters with a particular eye toward exploring issues of choice and response to the inevitable occurrence of disasters that, if not truly natural, have nature as a vital component. There are, as will be explained in the pages that follow, disasters that have critical elements that are intertwined with a multitude of human choices. In examining these disasters, we must take into consideration the role of human activity and choice in relation to these events' impact on human lives.

1

Optimism Interrogated
The Earthquakes and Tsunamis of 1755 and 2004

Nearly a quarter of a millennium separates two of the worst disasters that have confronted humankind: the 1755 earthquake and tsunami in the Atlantic Ocean and the 2004 earthquake and tsunami in the Indian Ocean. The timing of the disasters places them at opposing ends of the modern era of human development—an era characterized by our confidence in human ability to predict and control the happenings in the world.

Our entrance into and emergence from an era of modernity were shaped by shifting interpretations of optimism, which in turn affected how we responded to the disasters and crises we encountered. The 1755 earthquake and tsunami fell during a time when philosophers were beginning to wrestle with questions related to humankind's role in society. Central to many of their questions was the problem of how to integrate occurrences of human suffering into our understanding of the broader world. By 1755, Europe had endured periods of war, famine, and plague. For many people such occurrences provided cause for questioning how such tragedies fit into a broader vision God had for the world. For some, these questions were answered with a simple degree of faith in a notion that all things that happen to humankind—both good and bad—should be accepted as a reflection of benevolent will. Others, however, began to use the occurrence of these tragedies as part of a process for exploring our human potential to shape the world around us.

Two hundred and fifty years later, in December 2004, another earthquake and tsunami forced the world to reflect on another form of optimism. This latter form was grounded in beliefs of humankind's abilities to predict and prepare for any crisis encountered. The world had, according to this perspective, developed institutional and technological capabilities to aptly address many of the challenges that the world might confront. Through advances in science and economics, we could find ways to solve any problem, both foreseen and unforeseen, that we might encounter.

Both periods provide valuable lessons in how disasters are conceptualized and, ultimately, how responses to disasters are generated. A comparison of the periods helps us to explore how people in the stages of early modernity and people in the stages of late modernity might look to institutions to help address crises. In the case of the 1755 tsunami in Lisbon, for example, the nation-state was gaining relevancy over the Church as the central institution in society. As such, it was becoming perceived as the entity best positioned to wrestle with the challenges of disaster. In contrast, by the time of the 2004 tsunami, weaknesses of the nation-state in its ability to respond to crises were emerging. In the place of the nation-state were various nongovernmental institutions and nonstate actors that were becoming increasingly positioned to respond to crisis.

Each period also gave rise to notions of mutual assistance between nations and people living in them. In the 1755 earthquake and tsunami, the international response provided an early instance in which nation-states helped one another in addressing a crisis. At a time of intense competition between world powers for the positions of dominance in expanding colonial empires, a willingness to provide assistance to a competitor nation was a new phenomenon. In 2004, the global community engaged in cooperative relief efforts to a much greater extent than the world had witnessed before. These new dimensions of giving ultimately altered global expectations of how people's generosity might be drawn upon during a crisis.

I begin this chapter with an examination of concepts of optimism in Europe in the 1700s and link them to the 1755 earthquake and tsunami. I then examine the rebuilding and relief processes of the 1755 earthquake. I continue with an examination of factors of optimism as they emerged in the late twentieth and early twenty-first centuries, with an emphasis on the development of systems of prediction and perceived control. I conclude by linking much later notions of optimism to the tragedy of the 2004 earthquake and tsunami.

A comparison of these disasters provides a lens through which we can begin to examine other disasters and some of the shifts in thought that accompany them. We can explore frameworks of optimism that might exist and how they are contextualized at a given time. We can learn how such notions of optimism might be considered in light of possible disasters that populations in various parts of the globe may encounter.

OPTIMISM IN EUROPE

During the 1700s, an emergent concept within European Enlightenment circles was the notion of optimism. This belief held that God had a plan for all of humankind, and regardless of whatever catastrophes humankind might face, everything was both part of a larger plan and, regardless of the suffering it might cause, was meant to be good.

Central in the promotion of this concept were writers Gottfried Leibniz, Alexander Pope, and Voltaire. In his 1710 work *Theodicy*, Leibniz argued that all the imperfections of the world, including those that might seemingly cause harm, are part of God's plan. Alexander Pope, in his 1734 poem *An Essay on Man*, built on Leibniz's notions and suggested that since it is impossible for people to know all that underlies God's intentions, we need to merely accept that at the basis of all of God's intentions is a notion of good. Voltaire's perspective was best articulated in his 1733 *Letters Concerning the English Nation*, where he wrote that mankind should "thank the author of nature for informing us with that instinct which is forever directing us to futurity" (Voltaire 1741, 224). By assuming this approach to thinking about the gratitude that humankind should show God for granting us the mere ability to think about and aim for future goals, he acknowledged that it is important to accept the good and the bad that we might encounter.

By the late 1750s, however, Voltaire found himself in a position of criticizing the various proponents of optimism. Specifically, he found himself questioning the belief that it would be possible to merely accept the challenges that humankind encounters in the worst of catastrophes as simply a component of a divine plan. Much of the source for this level of criticism arose with Voltaire's struggle to make sense of the earthquake and tsunami of 1755.

PORTUGAL, 1755: AN EARLY-MODERN DISASTER

Portugal, like many other nations in the 1700s, was in the midst of determining its role in the broader European framework. The nation had begun establishing colonial interests in many of the corners of the world and was beginning to explore means of further exploiting much of the wealth that it was accumulating. Portugal's capital, Lisbon, was particularly known for its opulence, as much of the wealth generated from many of the Portuguese colonies in the Americas would end up in that city. Such wealth was, however, beginning to place Lisbon at odds with other nations of Europe, which were beginning to experience an increasing sense of competition with the Portuguese capital. It was also causing tension between the capital and many of the rural areas in Portugal that did not share in the capital's wealth.

Lisbon was also known as a city both steeped in Catholicism and still untouched by many of the Protestant reforms racing through much of the rest of Europe in the mid-1700s. To many people in the other cities in Europe, Lisbon was viewed as being permeated with Inquisition-era rituals, where the link between Christianity and idol worship had not been completely severed. As a result, its adopted forms of Catholicism were bound by an abundance of undertones that were in conflict with some of the Protestant perspectives that were emerging in various parts of the continent.

THE TSUNAMI

On the morning of All Saints' Day in 1755, many of Lisbon's parishes were full. Between 9:00 and 10:00 in the morning, several large tremors struck the city. Buildings around the city collapsed—including many of the churches where people had gathered for mass. Almost immediately, a series of fires erupted and began sweeping through the city. Caught in the middle of the falling rubble and fires, many of the survivors raced to the banks of the Tagus River in hopes of being able to cross to what was perceived to be firmer land.

About thirty minutes after the quake, many of the people who had gathered by the river watched as a previously unimaginable culmination to the events of the morning unfolded. The waters of the Tagus receded quickly and suddenly rushed forward in three subsequent waves that caught many of the people on the docks and riverside and dragged them out to sea. As one witness noted:

> On a sudden I heard a great outcry. The sea is coming in, we shall all be lost. Upon this, turning my eyes towards the river, which at that place is near four miles broad, I could perceive it heaving and swelling in a most unaccountable manner, as no wind was stirring. In an instant there appeared at some small distance a vast body of water, rising, as it were like a mountain, came on foaming and roaring, and rushed towards the shore with such impetuosity that tho' we all immediately ran for our lives, many were swept away. (Braddock 1755, 427)

The tragedy of the Lisbon earthquake was a direct challenge to those who followed the notions of optimism promoted by Leibniz and Pope. To simply dismiss the tragedy of Lisbon as part of a larger divine plan, as optimism would promote, seemed to discount the lives lost by the tragedy. A central figure among those questioning this notion of optimism was its former adherent, Voltaire.

In December 1755, Voltaire wrote a poem on the Lisbon earthquake as a direct challenge to the proponents of optimism. More importantly for him, it was a step in trying to build a context for understanding some of what had transpired. The poem attacked what he viewed as a blind sense of optimism being articulated by Pope, Leibniz, and others. In the preface to the poem, Voltaire wrote:

> If the question of physical evil has ever deserved the attention of all human beings, it is when these dreadful events occur, events that call

us back to the contemplation of our feeble nature, events like the great plagues that killed off one quarter of the population of the known world, the earthquake that swallowed up four hundred thousand people in China in 1699, those that happened in Lima and in Callo, and finally the earthquake in Lisbon and the Kingdom of Fez. The axiom that "All is well" seems a little off to those who witness these disasters. All is arranged, all is organized, doubtless by Providence; but it is only too apparent that All, for a long time now, is not arranged for our present welfare. (Voltaire 2000, 95)

Three years after the publication of his poem on the Lisbon earthquake, Voltaire published *Candide*, which he further used to criticize the notion of optimism. In *Candide*, Voltaire introduces readers to the teacher and optimist Pangloss and his student Candide. Both experience trials—however, with each trial Pangloss chooses to see only the good in a situation. All tribulations are merely part of a larger plan. Drawing upon the recollection of a witness of the tsunami, Voltaire depicted the following experience by Candide and Pangloss of the earthquake and tsunami in Lisbon:

Scarcely had they ceased to lament the loss of their benefactor and set foot in the city, when they perceived that the earth trembled under their feet, and the sea, swelling and foaming in the harbor, was dashing in pieces the vessels that were riding at anchor. Large sheets of flames and cinders covered the streets and public places; the houses tottered, and were tumbled topsy-turvy even to their foundations, which were themselves destroyed, and thirty thousand inhabitants of both sexes, young and old were buried beneath the ruins. (Voltaire 1901, 77)

The day following the events of the earthquake, fires, and tsunami, Pangloss shared with a group of the locals he and Candide met that the events of the previous day had to occur. "For," as Pangloss noted, "all this is for the very best end, for if there is a volcano at Lisbon it could be in no other spot; and it is impossible but things should be as they are, for everything is for the best" (Voltaire 1901, 79). This articulation reflected the perspective that greatly concerned Voltaire, one that suggested that a mere acceptance of a divine plan that includes the reality of the earthquake and tsunami of Lisbon should be the means of understanding and ultimately reacting to a disaster.

LESSONS FROM LISBON: ROLE OF GOVERNMENT IN DISASTER RELIEF

At the time of the 1755 earthquake and tsunami, Lisbon was in the midst of a political power transition. King John V had recently died, leaving power to his son Jose I. However, Jose I had little interest in governing a nation. Prior to his death, John V appointed Sebastian Jose de Carvalho e Melo, also known as Pombal, to head the Department of Foreign Affairs and War. Because of Jose's limited interest in matters of ruling a nation, he yielded a great deal of power to Pombal to manage the affairs of the state. A test of Pombal's governance abilities would come about in the aftermath of the earthquake and tsunami.

Central to Pombal's activities became the development of strategies for governing a nation managing in a state of chaos after its 1755 tragedy. Since the earthquake and tsunami raised a series of questions about how to respond to a disaster of the magnitude that struck Portugal in the mid-1700s, some of the strategies implemented by Pombal provided models for other nations. The Lisbon quake and tsunami provided one of the first instances when the nation-state would provide a foundation for the safety of its citizens. With these questions came an underlying assumption that the state would be capable of engaging in activity on behalf of its citizens and response would not be vested solely in the hands of the Church.

One of Pombal's first actions following the earthquake and one that helped to galvanize the role of the government in addressing people's needs was to appoint twelve magistrates—one for each of the twelve sections of the city, thus decentralizing the rebuilding process. Each of these magistrates had a distinct area they would be responsible for overseeing in terms of the administration of various relief services or items.

His second concern related to broad health considerations. Scattered throughout the city of Lisbon were corpses left as a result of the disaster. Officials feared that the number of dead people and animals lying in the streets would ultimately attract another wave of the plague, a crisis that Lisbon and many other cities in Europe had already endured several times. Pombal suggested that the fastest way to address this concern, was to collect all the bodies that could be found, load them onto barges, and sink the barges at sea.

RELIEF

News of the Lisbon earthquake and tsunami spread quickly through Europe. The stories of the destruction were met with a wide range of reactions. For some, the suffering of Lisbon called for provision of support for the citizens. Shortly after the Lisbon disaster, for example, the king of England sent a request to the English Parliament to respond in some way or another to the crisis. This early example of a disaster inspiring a nation to attempt to provide assistance for another raised a number of questions as to how nation-states might help one another at a time of need.

Support, however, did not come without its conditions. One of the prime areas of condition was a degree of moralizing regarding the state of affairs in Portugal. In 1755 theologian John Wesley published *Serious Thoughts Occasioned by the Late Earthquake at Lisbon,* in which he suggested that both Lisbon and London, which had suffered a minor earthquake in 1750, were showing signs of great evil. Three years later, he wrote a sermon entitled "The Great Assize," in which he suggested the earthquake would usher in God's New Kingdom. The quakes, in his opinion, were a sign from God of his displeasure in the conduct in both cities. In the case of Lisbon, its role as one of the centers for the Inquisition was of particular concern. As he noted regarding Lisbon's Inquisition linkages:

> Where so many brave Men have been murdered, in the most base and cowardly, as well as the most barbarous manner, almost every day, as well as every night, while none regarded or laid it to heart. (Wesley 1827, 165)

Ultimately, the 1755 earthquake and tsunami provided a framework for responding to a crisis that was unique, largely due to the broader societal changes occurring at the time. The nation-state's role was becoming more central. Nations were interacting with one another in very different ways than they had before. Intellectual frameworks were also emerging, largely as a result of many of the Enlightenment thinkers through whom to consider the changes and responses to disasters of enormous magnitude. However, the earthquake and tsunami also provided a critical lens for evaluating crises of the era. There were numerous lessons from the experiences in Lisbon that would help frame the perspective of how Lisbon might ultimately serve as a model for responding to a crisis of the magnitude encountered in the mid-1700s and might relate to the relief of disasters in the future.

A HISTORICAL FRAMEWORK: TWENTIETH CENTURY

Two hundred years following the 1755 tsunami, on April 1, 1946, an earthquake measuring 7.1 on the Richter scale struck the sea floor on the northern slope of the Aleutian trench. Within an hour, a hundred-foot wave struck Alaska's Unimak Island. Numerous scientists monitoring the quake assumed that the wave's impact on the ocean would dissipate in a relatively brief period of time. Five hours later, however, at 7:00 A.M. the Hawaiian island of Kauai was struck with several waves resulting from the quake. The waves demolished 488 homes, damaged 936 homes, and left 59 people dead (Atwater et al. 1999; Shepard et al. 1949).

In their 1949 assessment of the tsunami, Shepard and his colleagues recommended the development of a system of stations around the shores of the Pacific and mid-Pacific islands in order to watch for the arrival of tsunami waves. If a tsunami was detected, a report would immediately be sent to a central station that would in turn correlate reports and issue warnings to areas that lay in the path of tsunami waves. This would give residents in the tsunami's path adequate time to seek safety and shelter.

The Pacific Tsunami Warning Center, which resulted from this proposal, was located with the Honolulu Geomagnetic Observatory in Ewa Beach, Hawaii, in 1949. Initially, the center served primarily the mainland United States and the Hawaiian Islands, but service eventually expanded to cover a much wider area in order to protect other nations surrounding the Pacific Ocean.

Nearly twenty years following the launch of the Pacific Tsunami Warning Center, on May 22, 1968, one of the most powerful earthquakes recorded, at a magnitude of 9.5, struck off the coast of Chile. The quake generated one of the most destructive tsunamis—one that ultimately reached across the Pacific to Japan. Ultimately, the toll from both the quake and the tsunami was estimated at 2,300 people. As a result of the destruction and loss of life, scientists engaged with tracking and monitoring tsunamis would reaffirm their commitments to developing systems for monitoring and forewarning people of impending dangers from forthcoming tsunamis.

Thirty years later, in 1995, with newer technologies, the U.S. National Oceanic and Atmospheric Administration (NOAA) began implementing its Deep-ocean Assessment and Reporting of Tsunamis (DART) system to detect offshore tsunamis and better prepare coastal communities. The DART system is based largely on the existence of DART buoys, each of which is composed of an anchored seafloor bottom pressure recorder and a companion surface buoy. The bottom pressure recorder collects temperature and pressure data every fifteen seconds and transmits the data to the surface buoy. These measurements are then sent to the Tsunami Warning Centers, where the information is assessed, refined, and finally issued to the public in the form of tsunami watches, warnings, or evacuations. In 2000, six DART stations were deployed to strategic locations in the Pacific Ocean. By 2008, the DART network had expanded to thirty-nine buoys rimming the Pacific Ocean.

These systems provided a level of confidence for seismologists, oceanographers, and other scientists in the ability to be forewarned, in the Pacific Ocean at least, of an impending tsunami.

Optimism Shifted: 2004 Tsunami

"My family and I know that we have six hours," says Patra Rina. "If we do not see each other where and when we agreed, we know to let go of our expectation that we will meet." Patra Rina's arrangement with her family is one that she shares with people in her community of Padang City in West Sumatra, Indonesia, as part of the advice she provides on how to prepare for a tsunami. As executive director of a nongovernmental organization established to alert people about tsunamis, Patra Rina has found herself at the forefront of preparing her community for something that many of the people in her community feel is inevitable.

Prior to the morning of December 26, 2004, Patra Rina did not know what a tsunami was. "We learned quickly," she acknowledged, "and we learned that ultimately, we are not completely safe." Early that morning, the ground shook from what residents of Padang City thought was simply one of the many minor earthquakes the city feels every year. With an epicenter some 200 kilometers to the west of Padang City, far under the Indian Ocean, the perceived tremor was, in reality, a 9.0 quake on the Richter scale. The earthquake, which caused a rupture across nearly 750 miles of the ocean floor, led to a tremendous force of energy that sent water racing across the ocean at rates of up to 180 miles per hour. By the time the water reached land, many of the resulting waves were carrying crests of over 60 feet as they crashed into oceanside communities.

Fourteen nations had their coastlines impacted by the tsunami and, in some cases, witnessed a direct landing of the waves on coastal villages or towns. Other nations lost citizens who happened to be vacationing on beaches that were struck by tsunami waves and who, in some cases, were washed out to sea. In total, it is estimated that more than 250,000 people died and more than 1.7 million people were displaced as entire villages and towns in several countries were swept away in a matter of minutes.

The world responded—at least in the short term. Aid was pledged by governments around the globe, ultimately resulting in commitments of more than $13.5 billion. However, with nearly two million people without homes, tremendous loss of life, and the need to reconstruct communities at scales never before conceived, the various relief and reconstruction institutions needed to identify various strategies for rebuilding.

The tsunami of December 26, 2004, had a dramatic impact on how we conceptualize the realities of disaster in the early twenty-first century. Four areas in particular of our conceptualization surfaced. The first provided a critical lesson about the previously unimaginable. "This is an unprecedented global catastrophe and it requires an unprecedented global response," noted United Nations Secretary-General Kofi Annan several days after the tsunami. "Over the last few days, it has registered deeply in the conscience of the world" (Annan 2004). While communities in various parts of the world had experienced tsunamis, no records existed of any as widely devastating as the one that struck that morning. We learned from the images broadcast and the stories told, of both the tsunami and its aftermath, that nature does have the capacity to cause damage to previously unpredicted extents.

The tsunami also represented a shift in the roles of agencies engaged in responding to crises. No longer was it the state that would be assumed to be the primary respondent to a crisis or emergency. Instead, it became rapidly evident that in several cases, it was the nonstate actors that were engaged in the development of responses. In some instances, these nonstate actors were well positioned and empowered to respond to the crisis. In others, they were not. A new realization of what these actors might do, particularly in the context of governmental abilities and limitations, was a center of a discussion that echoed through the various policy-making bodies. These issues of recognizing potential disaster scale, the emergence of new actors, and the need for coordination structures between what had been a multitude of actors provides much of the legacy of the tsunami of 2004.

The role of science as a tool for predicting and reviewing crises was also brought to our attention by the tsunami of 2004. Prior to the tsunami, the Indian Ocean lacked a well-developed warning system comparable to the system in place in the Pacific Ocean. Following the disaster, however, several organizations began to develop plans to establish a Tsunami Warning System in the Indian Ocean. The success of the DART system in the Pacific has leveraged the hope that these early warning devices will prevent another disaster comparable to the 2004 tsunami.

Last, the tsunami shed light on the importance of coordination between and among national and international agencies. This became evident early on when reports and initial assessments of the tsunami began to be released. The most glaring weakness of these earliest reports was the clear noninvolvement of people in the affected communities in the collection of data and the development of approaches to rebuilding.

These issues of recognizing potential disaster scale, the emergence of new actors, and the need for coordination structures among a multitude of actors provide much of the legacy of the tsunami of 2004. An enhanced understanding of the realignment of global institutions, given these recognized issues, is a major component of what policy makers must take into account when looking at the inevitability of future extreme disasters and developing plans for response.

CONCLUSIONS

Comparisons between the 1755 tsunami in Lisbon and the 2004 Indian Ocean tsunami provide ample space for considering perspectives of optimism and conceptualizing many of the challenges of the twenty-first century. The impact of 1755 helped people to question the limits of benevolence and a sense of optimism, at a time when people were beginning to question what factors in the world order were within the bounds of human control.

The tsunami of December 26, 2004, had a dramatic impact on how we conceptualize the realities of disaster in the early twenty-first century. It provided a critical lesson about the previously unimaginable disaster. While communities in various parts of the world had experienced tsunamis, no records existed of any as widely devastating as the one that struck that morning. We learned from the images and the stories of both the tsunamis and their aftermath that nature does have the capacity to cause damage in previously unimagined extremes.

To coincide with the tenth anniversary of the 1995 earthquake in Kobe, Japan, the United Nations and other multinational agencies had already begun, months before the 2004 tsunami, to plan a meeting for early 2005 to explore strategies for enhancing response to crises and disasters. The timing of the 2004 tsunami illustrated the necessity of this meeting on disasters. Through the World Conference on Disaster Reduction held January 18–22, 2005, in Kobe, national and international actors explored the status of disaster risk reduction in the decade that had passed since the earthquake and established goals for the next decade for enhancing strategies for disaster risk reduction.

With a sense of purpose emboldened by much of what the world had experienced a few weeks prior to the meeting with the 2004 tsunami, the representatives from nearly 170 governments that gathered for the conference adopted a ten-year plan to make the world safer from natural disasters. Their plan, known as the Hyogo Framework for Action (HFA), emerged as a global blueprint for disaster risk-reduction efforts during the next decade. The primary goal of the Hyogo framework was to substantially reduce disaster losses by 2015 through the development of new institutions, approaches, and frameworks for enhancing response capabilities on a global scale. Whether the plans and goals developed through the Hyogo framework would help minimize the damage of further disasters of varying scales would be determined in the years to come.

2

Earthquakes and Progressive-Era Revival

Enrique Caruso's recital in San Francisco, which was part of a national tour of the Metropolitan Opera, was a performance that he had been anticipating for some time. For Caruso, then considered one of the most popular performers of the opera world, San Francisco would provide an opportunity to join many of the other major entertainers of his era in being able to list this rapidly growing West Coast city among the places where he had performed. For Caruso and many of his colleagues, San Francisco had grown in legend during a very short period of time. In only a few years, it had developed from a small encampment of miners drawn to the West in search of gold into a place that could claim to be the largest city on the West Coast of the United States.

Early in the morning of April 18, 1906, Caruso was awakened by the heavy rattling of his hotel room. He leapt out of bed and peered out of his window. What he saw were images of nightmarish proportions. Buildings to the left and right of his hotel had toppled, and people were running through the streets in a state of chaos. Within hours, Caruso was headed back to New York, where he commented a few weeks later that he never wanted to return to San Francisco. He never did.

The earthquake that Caruso and thousands of others experienced on that April morning would alter San Francisco's image in the view of much of the world. The excitement with which people would talk about this city would be tempered with stories of the 1906 great earthquake. For decades afterward, the San Francisco earthquake and fire would signify for many people the possible extremes of disaster in the United States.

In the early 1900s, San Francisco was a western model for Progressive-era growth, and it had many of the same challenges as the rapidly growing cities of the East Coast did in terms of population growth, immigration, public health, and housing. It also had many of the same questions related to matters of public safety that areas in the East and the Midwest were struggling with—in particular, how to manage challenges resulting from major disasters that might occur. Such public safety questions provide a foundation for exploring factors of rapid urban growth, the role of government, processes of rebuilding, and a multitude of other challenges that surface in relation to the relief and rebuilding called for by a catastrophe of the magnitude of the 1906 earthquake.

This chapter examines the 1906 San Francisco earthquake, with a framework that includes the multiple challenges that emerged from the quake of April 18 and the three days of fires that followed the quake. It takes into account many of the patterns of change and progress that were occurring in San Francisco in the early 1900s that help to frame the story of both the quake and some of the challenges of rebuilding that occurred in the years following the quake. I begin with an examination of San Francisco in the years prior to the earthquake—including the city's rapid population growth from the mid-1800s to the turn of the century. I continue with a presentation of the 1906 quake. I then examine the challenges and strategies that surfaced in the postquake era. The period of postquake rebuilding is particularly critical as a demonstration of the pressing challenges that may be faced as a community attempts to build back after a major crisis.

SAN FRANCISCO BEFORE 1906

The discovery of gold and the resulting movement of thousands of speculators to the San Francisco region in the late 1840s and early 1850s led to one of the fastest periods of migration in the history of the United States. Coupled with the development of businesses to support this growth, by the late 1800s San Francisco found itself one of the most rapidly growing cities in the nation.

In 1865 and 1868, two major earthquakes struck the city, providing residents of San Francisco an opportunity to think about how they would respond to earthquakes that might occur in the future. One of the survivors of the 1865 quake was a young writer by the name of Samuel Clemens, who had been in San Francisco documenting various experiences of people living in the West. In 1872, Clemens published a semi-autobiographical book entitled *Roughing It* about many of his experiences, including those in San Francisco during the 1865 quake. In the book, published under his pen name of Mark Twain, he noted:

> It was one which was long called the "great" earthquake, and it is doubtless so distinguished till this day. It was just after noon, on a bright October day. I was coming down Third Street. The only objects in motion anywhere in sight in that thickly built and populous quarter, were a man in a buggy behind me, and a street-car wending slowly up the cross street. Otherwise, all was solitude and a Sabbath stillness. As I turned the corner, around a frame house, there was a great rattle and jar, and it occurred to me that here was an item!—no doubt a fight in that house. Before I could turn and seek the door, there came a really terrific shock; the ground seemed to roll under me in waves, interrupted by a violent joggling up and down, and there was a heavy grinding noise as of brick houses rubbing together. I fell up against the frame house and hurt my elbow. I knew what it was, now, and from mere reportorial instinct, nothing else, took out my watch and noted the time of day; at that moment a third and still severer shock came, and as I reeled about on the pavement trying to keep my footing, I saw a sight! The entire front of a tall four-story brick building in Third Street sprung outward like a door and fell sprawling across the street, raising a dust like a great volume of smoke! And here came the buggy—overboard went the man, and in less time than I can tell it the vehicle was distributed in small fragments along three hundred yards of street. One could have fancied that somebody had fired a charge of chair rounds and rags down the through-fare. The street-car had stopped, the horses were rearing and plunging, the passengers were pouring out at both ends, and one fat man had crashed half-way through a glass window on one side of the car, got wedged fast and was squirming and screaming like an impaled madman. (Twain 1873, 421)

While incidents such as the 1865 earthquake were rare for cities, they did provide a basis for a major concern regarding safety in urban settings. Across the country, civic leaders were finding themselves concerned about both population increases and public safety in many of these cities. Much of the concern came with the recognition that as people continued to congregate in urban spaces, they confronted a host of new challenges related to their proximity to one another.

Issues of infrastructure development for the growth of San Francisco were of pressing concern, much of it focused on strategies for minimizing potential outbreaks of fires, a concern echoed in many other cities. In 1905, the National Board of Fire Underwriters published a report that included several recommendations on reducing fire hazards in cities, singling out San Francisco and noting in particular its faulty water distribution system as placing major parts of the city at risk. "San Francisco," observed the report, "has violated all underwriting traditions and precedent by not burning up. That it has not done so is largely due to the vigilance of the fire department, which cannot be relied upon indefinitely to stave off the inevitable" (Brearley 1916, 98).

SAN FRANCISCO AFTER THE 1906 QUAKE

Less than a year after the release of the National Fire Underwriters' report, the Pacific and North American tectonic plates lurched past one another. The movement of these plates sent shock waves at a rate of 7,000 miles per hour through the San Francisco region. For nearly 60 seconds, the ground quaked from southern Oregon to south of Los Angeles and as far east as central Nevada, covering an area of about 375,000 square miles.

"I hurried to Market Street—and what a sight!" wrote Charles B. Sedgwick, a newspaper editor and witness of the quake. He continued:

> It was a strange San Francisco that I gazed upon. I had seen this stately thoroughfare only the evening before . . . now the grand old street was scarcely recognizable—a sad scene of destruction. . . . Buildings by the dozen were half-down; great pillars; copings, cornices and ornamentations had been wrenched from the mightiest structures and dashed to the ground in fragments; the huge store window had been shattered, and costly displays of goods were so much litter on the floors . . . the sidewalks and roadway were covered with fallen stones, wooden signs and the wreckage of brick walls, the car tracks

were twisted, the roadbed had here fallen, there lifted, and everything on every hand was either broken, twisted, bent, or hideously out of place. (Sedgwick 1906)

As a result of the quake, gas and power lines were shaken and ruptured, setting off fires throughout the city. With its need to improve the water systems, San Francisco had a limited infrastructure with which its residents could fight the fire. As a result, for three days infernos swept through the city, burning anything that stood in the way.

Writer Jack London watched and reflected on the destruction that the city was experiencing:

> By Wednesday afternoon, inside of twelve hours, half the heart of the city was gone. At that time, I watched the vast conflagration from out on the bay. It was dead calm. Not a flicker of wind stirred. Yet every side wind was pouring in upon the city. East, West, North, and South, strong winds were blowing upon the doomed city. The heated air rising made an enormous suck. Thus did the fire of itself build its own colossal chimney through the atmosphere. Day and night the dead calm continued, and yet, new to the flames, the wind was often half a gale, so might was the suck. (London 2006)

By April 21, several days following the initial earthquakes and fires, the majority of fires were extinguished. In their place were nearly 500 incinerated city blocks and over 250,000 San Franciscans without their homes. Nearly 3,000 people were dead.

THE AFTERMATH

One of the most pressing concerns following the San Francisco earthquake was how to address the surge in the number of people displaced due to the earthquake and fires. In the first few days after the crisis, the number of people sleeping outdoors reached three hundred thousand. Many of them lived in temporary barracks built for short-term housing. Others lived in tents. In time, communities of evacuees, some with hundreds of people living in them, surfaced throughout the region. As one observer noted:

CHAPTER 2

The courage and energy of the population of San Francisco in the face not only of disaster but of extreme terror and sudden homelessness has not been exaggerated, but to a great many the full effect of the strain is not even yet apparent. The discomforts of living, in spite of adequate relief, are very great. Wind and fog—for the weather has been unusually cold for a month, dust unspeakable, cooking out of doors in camps and streets, lack of water for toilet appliances, the incessant boiling of water and milk for fear of fever, absence of light and means of transportation for some time—in short, the total uprooting of all the ordinary habits of life, is bearing more and more heavily on the women and children. Schools are closed, thus turning thousands of children literally into the ruined streets. It is now proposed to have a vacation school in Golden Gate Park for the children in camps there, but this is only a very small part of the whole number. . . . And for those who stay by the city much of this discomfort will go on for several months to come. That under such circumstances men and women become apathetic and lose pride and self-respect when they can no longer endure the strains of petty hardships, is not surprising. Archbishop Riordan, on his way to the scene of the disaster, is said to have predicted, as the worst effect of it, the deterioration of health and character which would be its inevitable result upon those who are not of the exceptional stuff of which heroes and pioneers are made. (O'Connor et al. 1913, 77–78)

With scores of people living in such closely enclosed encampments, many lacking basic sanitary needs, conditions were ripe for the outbreak of disease. The first sign that disease would emerge as a pressing concern was an increase in the number of flies in many of the camps. Well recognized as a source for the spread of typhoid, particularly with the presence of a large number of dead animals and amounts of waste piling up in many of the camps, flies were a worry for public health officials watching for the spread of disease. In the initial two months following the earthquake, the army counted ninety-five cases of typhoid. By mid-1907 more than one thousand cases of typhoid had been reported (Chase 2003).

Flies were not the only disease-spreading pests that surfaced during the recovery era in San Francisco. The shaking of the ground and the fires scared another population from their homes: rats. Throughout the city thousands of rats appeared and began to take advantage of the fact that many of the camps where people were relocated had piles of food scraps and other waste that they could forage through.

In late May 1907, a sailor on a tugboat known as the *Wizard* fell ill with a high fever. Within several days, he was dead from what later became identified as the *Bacillus pestis*, or plague bacteria. In August, a husband and wife fell ill after wrestling with their own encounters with the plague. At the same time, other cases were being reported to members of the medical community. By August, the plague began to appear in an increasing number of the camps in the San Francisco region. By the end of 1907, doctors had diagnosed 136 people who had been infected with the plague, and 73 of the cases proved fatal.

As Rupert Blue, who was then serving as a staff member of the U.S. Public Health Service and reported to Surgeon General Walter Wyman, observed:

> Rats abound in large numbers in the whole city, particularly in the burned district, where conditions for their maintenance are ideal. The ruins and piles of building material, and the broken and choked sewers form excellent nesting places, while the warehouses and uncollected garbage furnish an unlimited food supply. In addition, the houses for the most part are unprotected against the ingress of rats and other vermin . . . the section in which the foci are most numerous contain the refugee camps, which are built up in many places of shacks, and flea-infested cottages. The camps which are under the direction of the Relief Committee are in good sanitary condition, but they are in close proximity to the warehouses and broken sewers, which harbor large numbers of rats . . . There are still many pit latrines in use. . . . The city is very dusty. . . . The widespread area of the disease indicates that the campaign will be a long and expensive one, in which the available City fund will be rapidly expended. (Chase 2003, 156–57)

Thus, one of the critical lessons from San Francisco was that disease could surface in the aftermath of a major disaster. If San Francisco would be a guide for what challenges to expect following a crisis, it would provide lessons to consider as various health crises arise, and as people find themselves situated in whatever temporary encampments are established to assist with their shelter needs.

REBUILDING

Within hours of the earthquake, San Francisco mayor Eugene Schmitz met with a group of citizens at the San Francisco Hall of Justice to begin developing a strategy for rebuilding the city. For the assembled citizens there was no question as to whether to rebuild San Francisco. Many had invested in various arenas of San Francisco over the years and were eager to find ways to rebuild the value of their investments to pre-earthquake levels. Framing much of the needed conversation for them was the question of what strategies would be best for rebuilding the city and their investments.

The individuals gathered knew that one of the challenges San Francisco would face would be to fix perceptions that may have emerged from the quake. Across the country people were talking about the earthquake, with the fires added as an afterthought. To the people gathered at the Hall of Justice, the earthquake needed to be a second thought, particularly if they wanted to attract investors and new residents to the city. As a result, it was quickly decided that the tragedy of San Francisco would be presented as a tragedy of a fire and that there would be little official mention of the earthquake.

A week following the earthquake, the *San Francisco Chronicle* wrote of a meeting held by the San Francisco Real Estate Board, which passed a resolution declaring that the phrase "the greatest earthquake" should no longer be used. Events of April would be known only as "the great fire" (Hansen and Condon 1989, 11).

The concerns of the real estate board members mirrored the concerns of many business leaders who also wanted to downplay the risk related to the earthquake. They, too, positioned the disaster as a fire, recognizing that it would be easier to address people's concerns about fires than it would be to address their concerns about earthquakes. Fires are avoidable; earthquakes never are. As Stanford professor John Branner observed:

> Shortly after the earthquake of April 1906 there was a general disposition that almost amounted to concerted action for the purpose of suppressing all mention of the catastrophe. When efforts were made by

a few geologists to interest people and enterprises in the collection of information in regard to it, we were advised and even urged to gather no such information and above all not to publish it. 'Forget it,' 'the less said, the sooner mended,' and 'there hasn't been any earthquake' were the sentiments we heard on all sides. (Branner 1913, 2)

As he further observed:

No other and more serious obstacle is the attitude of many persons, organizations, and commercial interests towards earthquakes in general. The idea back of this false position—for it is a false one—is that earthquakes are detrimental to the good repute of the west coast, and that they are likely to keep away business and capital, and therefore the less said about them the better. This theory has led to the deliberate suppression of news about earthquakes, and even of the simple mention of them. Shortly after the earthquake of April 1906 there was a general disposition that almost amounted to concerted action for the purpose of suppressing all mention of that catastrophe. (Branner 1913, 2)

Geologist Grove Karl Gilbert noted in subsequent weeks a policy of "assumed indifference" in California regarding the danger of earthquakes:

This policy of assumed indifference, which is probably not shared by any other earthquake district in the world, has continued to the present time and is accompanied by a policy of concealment. It is feared that if the ground of California has a reputation for instability, the flow of immigration will be checked, capital will go elsewhere, and business activity will be impaired. (Gilbert 1909, 174)

Despite the efforts of many of the central figures in San Francisco's business community to present the disaster of 1906 as a fire and minimize its depiction as an earthquake, the city wrestled with major obstacles in carrying out this resolution. Part of the legacy of San Francisco is a focus on how we might think of crises in far more complex detail than they might be depicted. To view this merely as a crisis of fire, as many of the Progressive leaders of the era imagined they could, overlooks many of the complexities that shaped the responses to the crises, as well as long-term factors stemming from such responses.

Conclusion: The Legacy of the 1906 Quake

Despite the aims of many of the political and business leaders in San Francisco following the earthquake, the imagery of earthquakes in the twentieth century was shaped largely by the 1906 disaster. Part of the legacy of the 1906 quake and fire is asking the question of how to respond if a quake of such magnitude were to occur again. The lessons of the 1906 quake are useful as we consider plans for responding and rebuilding in the event of a catastrophe of similar or worse magnitude.

The denial that underscored much of the rebuilding process was a phenomenon we would see in the lead-up to and the aftermath of other natural disasters—where economic interest trumps open policy discourse that includes a frank assessment of all of the risks that come with a particular region.

The 1906 quake also helps to paint a picture of the complexities that might arise in a disaster. Housing and sanitation needs were a major concern in the aftermath of the San Francisco tragedy. Inadequate attention on solving these issues led to other challenges in the area of public health concerns. For decades following the 1906 quake, a question that San Francisco had to contend with was when would the next quake strike—and what type of damage might occur? In 1989 the region had a partial answer when the Loma Prieta quake struck the region, killed 63 people, and caused over $6 billion in damage.

Scientists predicting quakes, however, don't anticipate that Loma Prieta will have been the last major quake to strike the region. In 2003, the U.S. Geological Survey forecasted a 62 percent chance that, by 2032, an earthquake of magnitude 6.7 on the Richter scale will occur somewhere along one of the fault systems that are part of the San Andreas cluster that spear the Bay Area (USGS 2009).

Three years later, the *San Francisco Chronicle* explored the potential impact of a quake of the same magnitude as the 1906 earthquake striking the city of San Francisco today. According to the *Chronicle*, at least 3,400 people in the nineteen surrounding regions would die if the quake struck during the day when streets were filled. If at night, the toll would be over 1,800 people (Perlman 2006). The *Chronicle* also estimated that between 160,000 and 250,000 people would become refugees, and, over time, as many as 300,000 to 400,000 people would need to be relocated.

How well the nation and the region deal with such a crisis will largely be the result of planning and preparation practices and investments in infrastructure that can withstand some of the damage that would come with a disaster of this sort. Important, too, will be how well we will have learned from earthquakes of the past.

3

Limits of the Built Environment
Hurricanes and Choices of Locality

French colonialist Sieur de Bienville's justification for the site of the city he would found in 1718 was the location's proximity to both Lake Pontchartrain and the Mississippi River. While the benefits of these major bodies of water were numerous, particularly considering the transportation and agricultural possibilities they provided, there is little evidence that de Bienville considered the risks brought about by having the river and lake next to the city that would ultimately become known as New Orleans.

Four years after its founding, New Orleans was struck by the Great Hurricane of 1722 and was flooded by a swelling of the Mississippi River. All of the buildings in the new community were destroyed, and three of the ships that were sitting in the Mississippi were washed onto the river's shore. In response, de Bienville constructed a series of levees to manage the flow of water in the city in the event of future flooding.

The 1722 hurricane served as a harbinger of the future of New Orleans, and much of southern Louisiana, a region where sixty-five hurricanes have landed since the early 1700s, and every few years a hurricane of differing intensity strikes. Each time the region is stricken, residents opt to rebuild and hope they have better prepared communities for their next hurricane encounter.

Louisiana isn't alone in the extreme weather events it undergoes. Other states, particularly Texas, Florida, and North Carolina, have been hit by as many hurricanes, if not more, as Louisiana has encountered. In each of these areas the patterns are similar to those of people living in Louisiana: survive, rebuild, and aim to be better prepared for the next time a hurricane strikes.

This chapter examines hurricanes as disasters and some of the processes that communities have implemented to prepare for and respond to them. Much of the emphasis is on response in the form of adjustments in the built environment. I begin with an examination of the 1900 hurricane in Galveston, Texas, which remains on record as one of the worst disasters in the history of the United States. Galveston raises a critical question in our consideration of natural disasters—primarily whether when one considers the interplay between human choice, policy decisions, and risks, the Galveston disaster can truly be considered a natural disaster.

Slightly over a century after the Galveston hurricane, the world watched as waters flooded much of the city of New Orleans in the aftermath of Hurricane Katrina. Katrina was the result of not only weather; it was the result of years of policy decisions. Like the situation in Galveston, there were numerous questions about how factors of the built environment might have affected community safety.

The years between the Galveston hurricane and Hurricane Katrina were shaped by many of the patterns of migration to hurricane-prone regions. Government helped to encourage such movement through the advancement of initiatives that altered the natural environment or that enabled people to move to hurricane-susceptible areas. Ultimately, these incidents gave rise to numerous questions in the arenas of scientific prediction, assumed risk, and our locality choices.

GALVESTON

"The old Harris homestead where my aunts and my cousins lived was completely destroyed," Robert T. Jones recalled of his experiences as a seven-year-old in Galveston, Texas, in 1900. "I lost eleven relatives in the 1900 storm. I remember the mayor came in the next morning. He said to Father, 'John, your whole family is destroyed.' I remember that's the first time I ever saw Father with tears in his eyes" (Green and Kelly 2000, 169). Jones's recollection of the Galveston Hurricane is one of the dozens from survivors of what was one of the most severe disasters ever in a U.S. community.

Officially founded in 1825, Galveston was one of the fastest-growing cities in Texas. By the late 1800s, it had a population of over 35,000 people and had emerged as a critical port serving Texas and the states west of the Mississippi river. As the nation's leading cotton port, Galveston handled over 60 percent of the state's cotton crop in the mid- to late 1890s. In 1899–1900, it ranked third nationally in the export of wheat, sixth in cattle, and seventh in corn. This was a city with a tremendous amount of economic activity. Galveston, however, faces a number of risks from its geographic setting. It is situated among a curving chain of sand barrier islands two miles off the Texas coast, on an island that was, at its high point in 1900, only 8.7 feet above sea level, making it susceptible to extreme weather events such as hurricanes.

Galveston residents living on an island in the Gulf of Mexico at the end of the nineteenth century were not completely unaware of the risks they faced. In mid-September 1875, Indianola City, located further down the Texas coast, experienced a severe hurricane that destroyed three-fourths of the city and claimed approximately three hundred victims. A second hurricane hit Indianola on August 20, 1886, destroying what remained of the town. Having had their fill of storms, the remaining inhabitants abandoned Indianola.

THE STORM

The storms that wiped out Indianola in 1875 and 1886 led some members of the community in Galveston to wonder what types of protections their city should take against possible hurricanes. Some argued for constructing a seawall, and after a storm flooded several of the streets in July 1891, calls for such a seawall became greater.

One of the voices that argued against such a wall was Isaac Cline, the Weather Bureau's meteorologist stationed in Galveston. Cline's role in Galveston was the result of a recent merger between the Weather Bureau, which Congress had created the year before, and the Army Signal Corps, an entity created in 1870 under the presidency of Ulysses Grant. Cline's job in Galveston was to track weather changes and communicate by telegraph with Washington about any new developments in the nation's weather patterns. A component of Cline's work was to serve as a specialist regarding weather hazards in the local community. In response to the calls for a seawall, Cline argued in the *Galveston News*:

> . . . the opinion held by some, which are unacquainted with the actual conditions of things, that Galveston will at some time be seriously damaged by some such disturbance, is simply an absurd delusion and can only have its origin in imagination and not from reasoning. . . . It would be impossible for any cyclone to create a storm wave which could materially injure the city. (Larson 1999, 16)

In less than a decade, Cline would learn how wrong he was regarding the possibility of a major storm striking Galveston. On Tuesday, September 4, 1900, the Weather Bureau's Central Office in Washington, DC, telegraphed a message to the Galveston Weather Service of a tropical storm moving north over Cuba. The reports that followed varied in the quality of information on the storm that was known to be headed to Galveston within a few days. Early on the morning of September 8, Cline noted a significant change in the weather patterns. He telegraphed Weather Bureau headquarters in Washington to report "high waters with opposing winds never observed previously" (Green and Kelly 2000, 12). He then began to warn the city's residents.

On Saturday evening, September 8, 1900, the hurricane swept in from the Gulf with wind gusts of 120 miles per hour and a storm surge of 14½ feet. For the residents of Galveston, the combination of wind, storm surges, and flooding made the night of September 8 a time of fierce struggle. Cline noted in his recollections of that night:

> The battle for our lives, against the elements and the terrific hurricane winds and storm tossed wreckage lasted from 8 p.m. until near midnight. This struggle to live continued through one of the darkest of nights with only an occasional flash of lightning which revealed the terrible carnage about us. . . . Sometimes the blows of the debris were so strong that we would be knocked several feet into the surging waters, when we would fight our way back to the children and continue the struggle to survive. While being carried forward by the

winds and surging waters, through the darkness and terrific downpour of rain we could hear houses crashing under the impact of the wreckage hurled forward by the winds and storm tide, but this did not blot out the screams of the injured and dying. (Cline 1999, 96–67)

At minimum, it is estimated that the Galveston hurricane took the lives of over 6,000 people, the majority of whom were swept away in the waters of the Gulf of Mexico. Because of the large number of people who were lost in the Gulf waters, an exact number of those who died that night will never be known.

AFTER THE STORM

The morning light following the storm enabled survivors to survey the wreckage from the night before. A number of accounts describe a scenario with building remains and corpses scattered around the city. Charles Law, a traveling salesman who had come to Galveston a few days before the storm, wrote to his wife:

> On Sunday morning after the storm was over I went out into the streets and the most horrible sights that you can ever imagine. I gazed upon dead bodies lying here and there. The houses all blown into pieces; women men and children all walking the streets in a weak condition with bleeding heads and bodies and feet all torn to pieces with glass where they had been treading through the debris of fallen building[s]. And when I got to the gulf and bay coast I saw hundreds of houses all destroyed with dead bodies all lying in the ruins, little babies in their mothers arms. (Green and Kelly 2000, 25)

Despite Galveston's losses, city officials were determined to ensure that the city made a comeback.

In September 1901, the City Commission and the County Commissioners Court appointed a board of engineers to make recommendations to protect the city from future hurricanes. The engineers issued a report in January 1902, which called for the construction of a seawall—a barrier of reinforced concrete seventeen feet high, five feet wide, and three miles long—to shield the Gulf face of the city. In March 1902, the Galveston County voters approved a proposition to issue $1.5 million in bonds for the construction of the seawall. Work commenced in October, and the initial portion was completed in July 1903.

The second step was to raise the island to a greater height above sea level. The surge of water from the 1900 storm was almost twice the elevation of the land. A new company was formed to dredge watery sand from the harbor and pump it through pipes into city lots. When the water drained off, the sand remained, making the island higher. People lifted houses, buildings, churches, and even gravestones with jacks and poured the sand underneath. The task took nine years, but when completed, the company had raised five hundred city blocks with over sixteen million cubic yards of sand.

WEATHER PREDICTION AND CONTROL

The decades following the Galveston hurricane would witness tremendous advances in the field of meteorology. Many of these advances were driven by the needs of aviation, which would increase in importance in World War I, as pilots needed accurate predictions of weather to help ensure flight safety. This need for enhanced weather-prediction capabilities continued into the 1940s, when World War II added to the demand.

During the 1940s and 1950s, concern grew in Congress over the increase in the number of hurricanes affecting the United States each year. The concern reached a climax in 1954 when three major hurricanes—Carol, Edna, and Hazel—ravaged coastal areas from the Carolinas to Maine. The response was a recurring appropriation of funds, beginning in 1955, for research to deal with the annual threats from hurricanes. This infusion of new funds for programs to minimize loss of life and property led scientists and engineers to accelerate their efforts to find more effective means of predicting hurricanes and mitigating the damage that might come from them.

MIGRATION AND POSTWAR AREAS

In the 1950s and 1960s, an increasing number of Americans began to move into areas that were prone to hurricanes, such as coastal areas in Florida, Mississippi, Texas, and Louisiana. Population growth in many of these areas was driven by several policy decisions, economic realities, and technological developments. From a policy perspective, funding for highway construction as a result of the 1956 Federal Highway Act and other government sources of support ultimately enabled people to get to formerly remote coastal areas. In addition, postwar economic growth allowed them to begin purchasing new homes or to follow new job opportunities that were emerging in some of these areas.

Moves to coastal areas were also driven by the convenience that postwar modern life offered in many of these locations, which frequently had been difficult to inhabit in prior years. The increasingly widespread availability of air conditioning, for example, assisted in making areas previously considered physically difficult to live in, particularly during warmer months, livable through the year.

1960s: Donna, Carla, Betsy, and Camille

In early September 1960, Hurricane Donna ripped through Florida and its keys, sustaining winds of about 140 miles per hour and causing hundreds of millions of dollars in property damage. After the hurricane, the state commissioned a report to determine how buildings should be constructed to withstand hurricane winds. One of the concerns noted in the report was that builders had not taken ample steps to build structures strong enough to handle Florida's hurricane winds. The authors of the report noted that if growth in Florida continued at the rate it was projected in the early 1960s, there would be a great deal of havoc if a hurricane of Donna's intensity hit one of the state's areas with a projected higher population density.

In 1961, a year after Donna, Galveston had an opportunity with the arrival of Hurricane Carla to test its seawalls constructed in the early 1900s. To Galveston's good fortune, the seawalls held; however four hurricane-related tornadoes struck, destroying 120 buildings in the city and killing over forty people. In addition to being recognized for the destruction it brought to Galveston, Carla was the first hurricane to be covered live on television. As a result, viewers across the nation were able to witness the devastation as it was occurring and to better understand the intensity of hurricanes.

Four years following Carla, in September 1965, Hurricane Betsy, a Category 3 hurricane, made landfall in Louisiana and resulted in flooding from Lake Pontchatrain into New Orleans. Sections of New Orleans flooded as a result of several levee failures, including levees protecting major portions of the city's Lower Ninth Ward. Within this area, reports later appeared of residents drowning after being caught in their attics as flood waters rose.

Several days after Hurricane Betsy struck, President Lyndon Johnson visited New Orleans to view the hurricane damage. Following his visit to communities hit by the storm and its resultant flooding, he noted that the federal government would work with local officials to assist people as they rebuilt after the storm. As he noted:

> I have just completed an extensive tour of New Orleans and the surrounding area. I am saddened by the damage and the suffering that I have seen. The high winds that reached a speed of 145 miles per hour wreaked massive destruction. Roofs were crushed, trees toppled, tons of broken glass and shattered electric and telephone lines lay in the wake of the savage storm. Most of the city, as you observed, is still without lights this evening. With the winds came the rain, and untold misery has been caused by flooding. Many homes are now covered, including their roofs. But I am determined that we can help these people in every way that human compassion and effective aid can serve them. (Johnson 1965)

Hurricane Betsy was followed four years later by Hurricane Camille, which struck Mississippi's twenty-six-mile coastline on August 17, 1969. Camille moved across several states, including Louisiana, Mississippi, and Alabama. Numerous communities in Virginia were flooded by torrential rain from the hurricane. Camille's eventual death toll reached 256.

Donna, Carla, Betsy, and Camille influenced the field of hurricane preparation and response in two ways. First, they led to the development of means for measuring the severity of hurricanes. In 1969, Herbert Saffir, an engineer in Coral Gables, Florida, and Robert Simpson, then director of the National Hurricane Center, developed a classification process known as the Saffir-Simpson Damage Potential Scale in the aftermath of these hurricanes. Their scale was based on a myriad of criteria that predicted wind speed and indicated the likelihood of a storm surge. This new scale categorized hurricane rankings from Category 1, with winds of 75–94 mph, to Category 5, with winds in excess of 155 mph.

Second, the hurricanes justified a conversation on the issue of federal versus state response into areas of emergency relief. The severity of the 1960s hurricanes led many public officials to argue that there was a pressing need for the development of some unified means for responding to such disasters. This concern corresponded with other public safety concerns related to matters of civil protection that arose into the early and mid-1970s, leading President Carter to sign Executive Order 12148, establishing the Federal Emergency Management Agency (FEMA) in 1979. FEMA ultimately served to consolidate a half-dozen agencies responsible for civil defense and governmental operations for disaster relief. It would serve as the primary federal agency dealing with disaster relief.

ANDREW

In 1975, a Florida grand jury examination of building inspection processes in Miami–Dade County warned that the inspections were so poorly done that many structures could be blown away in a strong hurricane. "No excuse whatsoever can exist for the county to permit such inaction. Instead of requiring thorough, proper inspections, the county gave in to the pressure of the building industry," the report noted (Eleventh Judicial Circuit of Florida 1976). Ten years following the release of this report, the American Meteorological Society issued a warning about impending hurricane risks faced within the United States, noting:

> We are more vulnerable to hurricanes in the United States now than we have ever been in our history. . . . This statement is a plea for the protection of the lives and property of United States citizens. If we do not move forward quickly in seeking solutions to the hurricane problem, we will pay a severe price. The price may be thousands of lives. (American Meteorological Society 1986)

Four years later, in 1990, a second grand jury report accused regulators in Miami–Dade County of incompetence in the monitoring of building inspectors. "In too many instances, inspections are done too quickly or improperly in violation of department policy, or, in some cases, not at all," the report said (Eleventh Judicial Circuit of Florida 1990). Despite ongoing concerns regarding the ability of homes to withstand strong winds, inspectors continued to be lax in the reviews of buildings.

ANDREW STRIKES

In 1992, two years after the second grand jury noted its concerns regarding the quality of construction of homes in South Florida, and six years after the American Meteorological Society issued its warning about increasing hurricane risks, a tropical storm began to form off the coast of Africa. It crossed the Atlantic and by August 21 made a turn toward Puerto Rico, where it picked up strength and sped over the Caribbean Ocean. On August 24, 1992, it made landfall in South Florida.

With winds of about 145 miles per hour, Hurricane Andrew stands as the fourth most intense hurricane to make landfall in the history of the United States. The storm caused extensive damage in South Florida, and—after crossing the peninsula of the state—it entered the Gulf of Mexico and reintensified. It made landfall again near Morgan City, Louisiana, on August 26 as a Category 4 storm. The storm weakened quickly after its second landfall.

Andrew provided three critical realms for reflection on hurricanes. First, building code issues raised a major concern. In the months following Andrew, the *Miami Herald* launched an investigation into the building code standards in many of the areas impacted by the hurricane. During its investigation, the *Herald* analyzed 60,000 damage inspection reports for over four hundred South Florida neighborhoods. Reporters engaged in the investigations found several trends that raised many questions regarding the building code–approval process. Many of the neighborhoods that suffered the most destruction were some distance from the areas with the maximum winds; some of these neighborhoods were situated directly next to neighborhoods with minimal damage, and many newer homes—built after 1980—suffered greater damage than did older homes.

Second, Andrew provided an opportunity for the development of inquiries into the insurance arena. The estimated cost in property damage from Andrew was more than $30 billion. As a result, various agencies began to develop means of minimizing exposure to areas such as those in coastal zones. For example, in late December 1993, the *New York Times* reported that some insurance companies were implementing a process known as "shore-lining," a term for refusing to provide coverage to customers with homes within five thousand feet of a shore (Quint 1993).

A third major concern that arose in the aftermath of Andrew was the proper role of FEMA. Specifically, what might FEMA do, and how might FEMA's efforts be undertaken with more positive outcomes? FEMA's degree of authority surfaced as an area of concern—particularly the perception that it needed to wait for specific requests from states before being able to provide assistance. FEMA should clarify and expand its authority to act quickly after major disasters, rather than wait for specific requests for aid from the states.

Andrew's lessons, from building code factors, to issues of local versus federal government roles in disaster relief, to insurance concerns, added to the complexities that made Andrew at the time the costliest hurricane in American history. Within a little over a decade, that distinction would change.

KATRINA

"Filling the bowl" was the name of the scenario presented by reporters John McQuaid and Mark Schleifstein in a 2002 five-part *New Orleans Times-Picayune* series on hurricanes in southern Louisiana. In the series, McQuaid and Schleifstein examined various scenarios that would be confronted if at some point New Orleans were struck by a major hurricane and the city were to flood. In the "filling the bowl" scenario, water would flow over the levees of Lake Pontchartrain into the city, ultimately flooding major sections. People would be stranded in floodwaters contaminated by various toxic wastes, at risk of electrocution due to downed power lines, and stuck on the roofs of their houses hoping for rescue.

McQuaid and Schleifstein predicted a surge in the need for temporary housing for the possible one million evacuees who would be in desperate need of housing in the aftermath of such a scenario. As they noted:

> New Orleans would face the future with most of its housing stock and historic structures destroyed. Hotels, office buildings and infrastructure would be heavily damaged. Tens of thousands of people would be dead and many survivors homeless and shellshocked. Rebuilding would be a formidable challenge even with a generous federal aid package. (McQuaid and Schleifstein 2002)

McQuaid and Schleifstein's series took into account the reality that southern Louisiana has undergone a number of environmental shifts over the past several decades—most of them largely the result of human activity. For thousands of years, tons of silt have amassed throughout the region, consisting of topsoil carried largely by the Mississippi River from states to the north. Much of southern Louisiana is made up of delta lands created by this relocated topsoil.

When the Army Corps of Engineers began building the levee and canal system along parts of the Mississippi River, partially in response to the floods of 1928, the amount of river sediment began to change, creating major geographical changes that have increased the regional susceptibility to hurricanes.

One of these geographical changes for Louisiana over the past several decades has been a loss of its wetlands. In 1950, the state still had the vast majority of the wetlands that had greeted the Sieur de Bienville in 1718. However, since 1950, a number of changes in the built environment—including the construction of more dams, levees, and canals—have caused the wetlands to vanish in increasing amounts.

One culprit in the destruction of many acres of wetlands in the region is the oil industry. Since the early 1900s, thousands of exploratory and development wells have been drilled in Louisiana's eight coastal parishes. Since the late 1930s, additional canals and pipeline corridors were built and drilling barges were moved into the marshes. These changes have led to making what was already an ecologically fragile region far more susceptible to extreme weather events.

THE HURRICANE AND ITS AFTERMATH

In July 2004, two years following the McQuaid and Schleifstein series, a team of over 250 representatives from a number of government agencies gathered in New Orleans for a FEMA-funded simulation exercise known as Hurricane Pam. The primary assumption underlying the Pam scenario was that New Orleans would be inundated with ten feet of water due to failures in its levee system after a Category 3 or stronger hurricane struck the city. One of the conditions presented under Pam was that it would not be just water, but a toxic waste mixture that would flood the various communities, largely as a result of New Orleans' having been home to numerous toxic waste sites.

Less than a year following the Pam exercise, in late August 2005, residents of New Orleans began to receive forecasts of a hurricane named Katrina with 145 mph winds that was sweeping into the Gulf of Mexico region. On August 29, 2005, it struck land. By ultimately devastating 90,000 square miles along the Gulf of Mexico, Katrina served as one of the first major natural disasters of the twenty-first century.

In New Orleans itself, the morning after Katrina allowed many of the residents who remained in the city to breathe a momentary sigh of relief. Katrina had missed a direct landing on New Orleans, so for many people, the city had escaped what they viewed as a potentially catastrophic situation.

Within a matter of hours the feelings of relief were replaced by sudden feelings of panic. Katrina had caused some breaks in the levees that were protecting the city, and within a matter of hours, much of New Orleans was flooded.

For weeks, the images of Katrina broadcast across the nation demonstrated how unprepared the nation was for a disaster of this size, a disaster that had been predicted. We saw hundreds of people crammed into the Louisiana Superdome, one of the places of refuge for those who fled their homes but were not able to flee the city. We saw images of major sections of the city flooded, leaving people stranded on their rooftops or, worse, trapped in their attics. We heard of the challenges faced by members of the police force who struggled with understaffed resources to maintain some semblance of public order in a chaotic situation.

Central in many of the conversations regarding Katrina was how the city fared in evacuating its hundreds of thousands of residents. Questions arose about the coordination of evacuation processes in the time following Katrina. Why weren't more people evacuated? Did the plans for enabling evacuations overlook the poor or the elderly residents of the city? What type of power did the city or state have to forcibly remove people who did not wish to evacuate? In the time that followed, there were also questions regarding how and where people would be resettled in the coming years.

One critical concern related to issues of resettlement in the wake of the tragedy was how, in the short and long term, temporary housing needs would be managed. In many parts of the country, particularly in various communities in the South, Katrina trailer parks were established as short-term locations for housing people. In Louisiana alone, 48,000 trailers and mobile homes were deployed for families that had been displaced by Katrina. Some of these trailers were placed in clusters with other trailers, in short-term parks or other settlements. Regardless of how they were set up, the trailers came to represent for many people the tremendous task of rebuilding that the region would need to face in the years to come.

Ultimately, the trailers and the other visual reminders of Katrina pointed to questions that the city has faced since the hurricane and flood of 1722. Should New Orleans be rebuilt? Or, given what is known about the risks of the region, should people abandon the idea that through adaptation of the built environment, New Orleans could be made fully safe from extreme weather events like the hurricanes that are interwoven in the city's history?

REBUILDING

Five years after Katrina, the Army Corps of Engineers was pouring the final concrete into a rebuilt system of levees. This new system cost nearly $15 billion and included a 350-mile system of levees, floodwalls, gates, and other structures (Schwartz 2010). The completion of the levees was an indication that as far as residents of the city were concerned, New Orleans would be rebuilt.

The statistics from Katrina became clearer in the years since the hurricane. Over fourteen hundred people had died in the hurricane and subsequent flooding. Half a million homes had been damaged or destroyed in Louisiana, and more than one million residents of the Gulf Coast had been displaced. One hundred thousand of those who had been displaced did not return to the state.

CONCLUSION

According to the National Oceanic and Atmospheric Administration (NOAA), by 2025, 75 percent of all Americans will live within fifty miles of a coast. As a result, a large percentage of Americans are vulnerable to extreme weather events such as hurricanes (Restore America's Estuaries and NOAA 2002). In the cases presented, I have examined some of the challenges associated with the assumptions underlying factors of locality where, in the late-modern era, possibilities of extreme weather occurrences are very real.

Numerous lessons can be drawn from previous experiences with extreme weather coastal disasters that will help us as we prepare for future disasters. Central are issues of location. By situating communities in vulnerable locations or rapidly rebuilding in areas that are susceptible to extreme weather events, are we ultimately creating risks at national, state, and local levels that may not be in our best interests? Are there strategies for encouraging migrations to less disaster-prone areas? Or do we simply need to do a better job of reinforcing the built environment for standing up against disasters that we might anticipate, even if only remotely feasible?

Like other natural disasters, the inevitability of hurricanes is a fact. What is not inevitable, however, is extreme destruction in their wakes. Questions of location, risk mitigation, and historical frameworks for understanding processes are critical to understanding mechanisms that might emerge to ameliorate the effect of hurricanes.

Also critical are issues of the built environment in relation to hurricane reduction. Galveston provided a critical example of restructuring the natural landscape with its seawalls and land elevation to better frame the prospects of the built setting. New Orleans provided another example with its building of levees. As increasing numbers of people move to locations near water, and as questions about the development of the built arena arise, we will need to deal with increasing challenges of protecting rising population bases in the paths of extreme weather events.

Part II

Global Public Health

In March 1677, the Royal Society's *Philosophical Transaction* published a letter written by a Dutch shopkeeper named Antony Leeuwenhoek. Untrained in the medical sciences but the inventor of numerous microscopes, which he used to peer at items much too small for the unaided human eye to see, Leeuwenhoek described creatures that he had discovered while looking in raindrops he collected. He noted "these little animals to my eye were more than ten thousand times smaller than . . . the water-flea or water louse, which you can see alive and moving in water with the bare eye" (Friedman and Freidland 1998, 41). Over the years, additional submissions to the Royal Society by Leeuwenhoek helped to establish further evidence of a microscopic world and provide a foundation for what would become the field of microbiology.

It would not be until the middle of the 1800s that linkages between Leeuwenhoek's work and the spread of disease would be explored at further length through the development of new hypotheses and new discoveries in microbiology. In 1840, German physician and anatomist Jakob Henle built upon the work of Leeuwenhoek and wrote an essay entitled *Miasms and Contagia*, which articulated one of the first clear statements that infectious diseases are due to specific microorganisms. The work of Leeuwenhoek and Henle provided critical junctures in the development of our understanding of the cause and transmission of infectious disease. Their advances were coupled with new stages in the understanding of how diseases develop and the cycles surrounding them.

In the 1860s, Louis Pasteur proved that bacteria were living organisms that replicated and that they did not emerge from some means of spontaneous creation, as was commonly believed at the time. His work led to what became known as pasteurization, a means by which foods and liquids are heated and rapidly cooled to minimize the presence of pathogens. In the 1870s Pasteur further advanced the field of bacteriology by identifying a way to provide inoculations of smaller doses of disease to prevent later infections, thus formalizing a technique of vaccination.

Ultimately, Pasteur's work, building upon that of Leeuwenhoek, ushered in an era during which concepts of germ theory were understood as being critical for minimizing the spread of infectious disease. This work suggested a major shift in how we thought about disease in various settings. Increasingly, we found ourselves in an era in which the notion of germs became central to the cause of diseases as we perceived them. The period ultimately was referred to as the "golden era" of microbiology, an era when scientists, with their increasingly powerful microscopes, were able to isolate the causes of various diseases and over time develop strategies for responding to them.

These developments helped to build a new framework for appreciating advances in the field of global public health. Prior to the work of such figures as Leeuwenhoek, Henle, and Pasteur, we remained largely ignorant of the role of germs in causing diseases. This new foundation of knowledge ultimately helped to build an understanding of both science and medicine that would shape how we responded to infectious disease.

The period also had an effect on the development of systems and institutions at local, national, and international levels to deal with matters of public health. Knowing about germs and ultimately viruses, we were able to address the systems that enable their growth, and through new health controls and sanitation measures, we could develop means to minimize their impact.

Finally, the period also provided a foundation in scientific knowledge that enabled us to wrestle with challenges of broader questions related to science and society. Our advances in science helped us to implement various strategies for advancing our knowledge about medicine and the ultimate reduction of transmittable infectious disease.

This section examines crises of global public health with an emphasis on the balance of our knowledge of infectious disease and the implementation of standards to control for threats caused by such disease. I begin with a historical examination of patterns of response to the cycles of plague that ravaged Europe from the mid-1300s to the mid-1700s. This examination provides an overview of disease as both an accelerator of social change and a departure point for examining responses to later public health disasters driven by infectious disease. As a coinciding component to the plague, people began to challenge many of their basic assumptions about matters such as the role of religion, science, and medicine in the broader society. As a result, changing ideologies provided a foundation for many of the later advances in science and society, ideas that resulted in the progressions marked by later periods such as the Enlightenment, the modern era, and the late-modern era.

I continue by examining some of the early work related to germ theory and epidemiology, which helped to frame some of the processes and protocols for tracking and managing the spread of infectious disease. Through an examination of work in the fields of epidemiology and public sanitation, I analyze perspectives on early public health strategies that could support means of identifying the sources for the cholera epidemic in London, one of the major health crises of the mid-1800s and one that ultimately changed our thinking about how to minimize the spread of infectious disease in later years.

The assumptions underlying progress in epidemiology met a major challenge in the latter years of World War I with the emergence and spread of the pandemic influenza of 1918. This pandemic, which is the focus of the next chapter, ultimately led to the deaths of over twenty million people around the globe and became the benchmark against which we would frame discussions about medical advancement in later encounters with the flu and other infections.

For over sixty years following the 1918 flu, there were a number of advances in global public health that ultimately led to renewed assumptions about the potential progress that medical science could make in battles against infectious disease. There were also several institutional frameworks that emerged to help address these outbreaks. In particular, the launch of major health campaigns to suppress polio, smallpox, and malaria are an example of some of the major advances and the optimism related to medical progress in the era. This period was also one in which several of the medical and scientific institutions that focused on enabling medical progress were developed. Most importantly, they helped to instill a sense of belief that medical knowledge, coupled with entities such as the Centers for Disease Control and the World Health Organization, would enable us to defeat medical challenges that might arise.

This sense of confidence, beginning in the early 1980s, would confront one of the major challenges that the global medical community would face: the rise of HIV/AIDS. In just slightly over three decades, HIV/AIDS would become responsible for taking millions of lives around the globe and forcing nations to consider the broader societal impact when large segments of the population are affected by such a disease. In some nations where more than one-fourth of the population was believed to be HIV positive, concerns about the broader impact on labor availability, economic output, and changing social service needs were central in policy dialogues. HIV/AIDS signaled that our perceived medical advances would still confront numerous challenges in the area of infectious disease.

The latter years of the twentieth and the first decade of the twenty-first centuries witnessed the rise of new infectious diseases. These outbreaks brought to light various challenges as medical and scientific researchers began to consider the possible scenarios that could emerge from an unprecedented urbanization, realities of air travel, and interspecies viral adaptation—all of which serve as major components of present-day infectious threats. The final chapter of this section explores the realities of these threats of infectious disease in this late-modern era, using the experiences of the emergence of severe acute respiratory syndrome (SARS) as a case study.

Ultimately, the crises of infectious disease and public health that are included in this section provide a foundation for exploring specific public health threats and the institutional responses related to them. The lessons drawn from history, stretching as far back as the years of the plague, provide a context for considering the various threats of infectious disease, the various institutional responses, and the challenges to institutional development that underscore how we respond to the complexities of public health and evolving challenges of infectious disease. It also raises several questions about the interrelations between scientific and medical progress and the complications that surface with such progress.

4

Plague as Crisis and Corollary to Societal Change

"Inow began to consider seriously with myself concerning my own case, and how I should dispose of myself; that is to say, whether I should stay in London or shut up my house and flee, as many of my neighbors did," noted the narrator of Daniel De-Foe's 1722 *A Journal of the Plague Year* (Defoe 1896, 11). This novel, which depicts the experience of living in the time of the bubonic plague in London 1665, stands as one of the strongest accounts of the plague of that era. Based largely on recollections and notes believed to be from DeFoe's uncle, *A Journal of the Plague Year* appeared at a time when fears of the Plague of Marseilles of 1720 and 1721 were appearing throughout Europe.

Many of the English fears of the plague of the 1720s were shaped by stories of the plague of the 1600s that had passed from one generation to the next. Whether from the visual image of people suffering from the maddening pain of boils appearing all over their bodies, or the loss of mind as the plague-causing *Yersinia bacilli* attacked the brains of the victims, the effect was panic among all who heard stories from the survivors. These images of the physical impact on people were coupled with tales of social and economic unrest as existing forms of government and business unraveled as a side effect of the plague.

History has provided several recollections of plague periods in the world. Our comprehension of these recollections provides a foundation for understanding the various responses to the spread of infection and disease.

Ancient records depict the perceptions of many cultures that plagues were linked to demonic influences. Babylonian myths from over three thousand years ago, for example, depict the periodic emergence of Namatar, the demon of plague and other epidemics, as playing a major role in the spread of plague and pestilence. During the Irish pestilence of 1084, legends arose of demons who released flames from their throats as they spread the plague.

While there are numerous stories of plagues from various parts of the ancient world, our first collective historical recollection of battles with the plague is of the one that struck the world in cycles over the course of two hundred years, beginning in roughly 540. Most commonly known as the Justinian Plague, it is believed to have begun somewhere in Southwest Asia and spread throughout much of Asia and Europe. The magnitude of the plague is described by Procopius, who, in his *History of the Peloponnesian War*, describes a rate of 10,000 deaths per day at Constantinople, where, according to him, half of the inhabitants of the Byzantine Empire were dead by A.D. 565.

History also provides us with an important lens for reflecting upon our experiences with various diseases. Plague has come to serve as a metaphor for any major pandemic that humankind finds itself confronting. We know that when the concept is mentioned, we are talking about far more than just the spread of an illness that will impact dozens or even hundreds; the cultural and historical connotation of the word conveys that we are talking about death on a catastrophic level—one that could affect thousands, if not millions, of people. As a result of the gravity with which we associate the term, we know to consider the health impact of plagues and many of the broader societal questions that arise from them.

The four-hundred-year period stretching from the mid-1300s to the mid-1700s when the concept of plague emerged, subsided, and reemerged, coincided with tremendous change on the European continent. At the beginning of this four-century period, Europe was in its later Middle Ages and wrestling with cycles of famine that depicted a near Malthusian reality where population growth nearly overshadowed the availability of resources necessary for subsistence. At the end of the period, the continent was about to undergo its period of Enlightenment and the very beginnings of a modern era, which would ultimately shift European societies—and the societies they influenced—in ways that would dramatically alter the course of humankind's historical progress. Many of the societal transitions occurring during this era were driven by major transitions in the areas of science, education, and governance, which in turn helped to facilitate the emergence of modern society.

Three eras are critical for this examination of Europe's plague years and their impact on periods of modernity and late modernity. The first is in the 1340s, when, by some estimates, over a third of Europe's population fell victim to the plague. This initial era had Europe both depopulated and psychologically shattered due to such rapid population loss. Such shocks ultimately helped to trigger several shifts in population and mindset that launched several of the initial transitions that helped to move Europe into its Renaissance era, when numerous discoveries would be made in the sciences and the arts and ultimately lead to later transitions in human progress.

The second critical plague period examined, which occurred in the 1660s, saw the beginning of changes that prompted the emergence of the patterns that led to an era of Enlightenment and its political and scientific precursors to a modern era. In England particularly, this second period of plague led to a transition in thought in governance and science that would provide a foundation for the Enlightenment philosophers several decades later. These philosophers would in turn validate perspectives that would lead to an era of early modernity with its various notions of scientific progress and self-determination.

The third period examined took place during the 1700s, when England, in response to the crisis of the plague in Marseilles during the 1720s, instituted a number of policies that signaled new strategies for prevention. Parliamentary laws framed policy responses to help control the conditions caused by the plague. This period, and England's reaction to this last stage of plague in Europe, demonstrated a shift in ideology marked by people's belief that they could control their own destinies in regard to the plague.

Ultimately, each of these periods provides a view of the interplay between this aggregated period of crisis and the broader society. These periods helped to create a foundation over the years for shaping new thought paradigms that would lead to both the modern and late-modern eras, their corresponding stages of advancement, and the various societal risks and crises that would come with such challenges.

THE PLAGUE: 1300s

In the early 1340s, fleas infected with the *Yersinia pestis* bacteria are believed to have infected millions of rodents in Mongolia. As the infected rodents and the fleas they carried made increasing inroads into human areas for food, they brought with them the bacteria, infecting increasing numbers of people. The impact was devastating. The population in China is estimated to have been roughly 123 million in the year 1200. Nearly two hundred years later, in 1393, numerous cycles of plague had decreased that number to roughly 65 million.

Within a few years, much of Europe began to hear rumors of the magnitude of death throughout Asia, particularly in parts of China. By the late 1340s, rats carrying the fleas infested with the bacteria arrived in Italy on ships that had returned from the Crimean Sea. These rats, along with migrating people, helped to introduce the bacteria into new populations throughout Europe. As was the case in China, the impact in Europe was devastating.

On a large scale, many historians believe that between 1346 and 1350, at least one-third of Europe's total human population (20–30 million people) died of the plague that resulted from the widespread introduction of the *Yersinia* bacteria into the continent. On a local level, the statistics were just as staggering. London lost 35,000 of its original 60,000 inhabitants, and Venice lost 90,000 of its residents out of a population of 150,000 in slightly over eighteen months. Paris had a daily death rate of 800 people, and Pisa found itself losing 500 people per day (Herlihy 1997).

Throughout Europe, these drastic shifts in population and the fear and anxiety caused by the plague brought about tremendous change in the lives of people in the infected areas. Many of these shifts indirectly helped place humankind on its path toward modernity and its corresponding notions of determinism, scientific progress, and technological capability that shaped much of modern and late-modern thought.

With one-third of Europe dying as a result of the plague, many people wrestled with questions related to the broad role of religion and the church in society. Traditionally people had thought of the church as the intermediary between themselves and God. It was supposed to convey both God's messages to the people and the people's concerns and desires to God. With thousands of people dying in cities and towns across the continent, scores of people wondered where God was in helping to alleviate humankind's suffering from the plague. Where was the church in its role as an intermediary with God? Was God angry with man and permitting the plague to occur as some form of punishment for his sins? As one English cleric wrote:

> Terrible is God toward the sons of men . . . and by his command all things are subdued to the rule of his will. Those whom he censures and chastises; that is, he punishes their shameful deeds in various ways during this mortal life so that they might not be condemned eternally. He often allows plagues, miserable famines, conflicts, wars and other forms of suffering to arise, and uses them to terrify and torment men and so drive out their sins. And thus, indeed, the realm of England, because of the growing pride and corruption of its subjects, and their numberless sins . . . is to be oppressed by the pestilences and wretched moralities of men which have flared up in other regions. (Horrox 1994, 113)

If the church was seen as the institution that served as a liaison between humankind and God, then the impact of such a major pestilence delegitimized the church's ability to serve as such a conduit. Thus, the crisis was not so much one of lost faith in God. Rather, it was a crisis of legitimacy for the church and its perceived role as an intermediary between people and their God.

The plague also had an impact on the makeup of many of the religious orders throughout Europe. Many of these orders were limited in the frequency and scope of interactions their members could have with people from the outside world. On a positive side, this served as an occasional barrier to new infections. On a negative side, it would prove problematic when a community became infected and the infection spread rapidly among its members. St. Francis's Abbey in Kilkenny, Ireland, was one of hundreds of religious communities that was losing many of its members to the plague. One community member, Friar John Clyne, observed:

> That pestilence deprived of human inhabitants villages and cities, and castles and towns, so that there was scarcely found a man to dwell therein; the pestilence was so contagious that whosoever touched the sick or dead was immediately infected and died; and the pestilence and the confessor were carried to the grave . . . many died of boils and abscesses, and pustules on their shins and under their armpits; others frantic with pain in their head, and other spitting blood; . . . waiting for death till it come . . . so I have reduced these things to writing; and lest the writing should perish with the writer, and the work together with the workman, I leave parchment for continuing the work, if haply any man survive, and any of the race of Adam escape this pestilence and continue the work which I have commenced. (Carrigan 1905, 106)

The plague's devastation of religious communities generated a discussion on how replacements for members of religious orders would be found. As a result, investments were made in the development of several institutions where new priests and members of religious orders would be trained to replace those who had fallen victim to the plague. Some of these institutions were the result of bequests from people who died of the plague, to benefit poor scholars, future priests, and the institutions that trained them. Thus Cambridge University acquired four new colleges, the foundations of which can be attributed to the plague. Oxford acquired two new colleges. In at least one case, the founding Bishop of Trinity Hall specifically noted that the purpose of the development of the new college was to replace the losses that the clergy in England had suffered (Ziegler 1971).

Many of these universities were far from home for many of the potential scholars. In an era of plague possibilities, one concern was for students to have opportunities to engage in religious and academic studies closer to home, rather than having to travel through territories that might have higher rates of plague. As a result, several local universities were founded in various cities throughout the continent: in 1348, Charles University in Prague; in 1365, the University of Vienna; in 1386, Heidelberg University.

This increase in the number of universities as locales for learning also in time provided a basis for thinking about various disciplines of study besides theology. For years prior to the out-break of the plague in the 1340s, medicine had been grounded in the philosophy of Galen of Pergamon. According to him, one's health was the product of different types of humors in the body: blood, phlegm, yellow bile, and black bile. Every person had a unique balance of humors, and a doctor's job was to determine when those humors were out of balance and prescribe a proper treatment to rebalance them. Normally, according to this medi-cal approach, humor imbalance, which was the cause of illness, was due to vapors in the air. Treatment for illness consisted of anything from changing the amount of sleep one would get, to altering one's diet, to eliminating certain activities perceived as making one susceptible to such imbalances.

The inability to treat the plague during the medieval era with methods based on Galenism led medical practitioners to pursue studies of the human body. In many cases, these approaches ran counter to what the church considered permissible. Many practitioners began incorporating the dissection of cadavers into their research, a practice that was prohibited throughout much of the continent by the church, and thus further challenged the legitimacy of the church and its rule. These activities and the ad-ditional knowledge that resulted about the human body would in time lead to new understanding of human anatomy. These approaches also demonstrated an increasingly prevalent belief that human actions in the area of medicine—and not necessar-ily divine intervention—could play a critical role in developing solutions to medical challenges.

Medieval European economic activity was also affected by the plague. The deaths of thousands among the peasant class ulti-mately had a significant impact on the labor pool, and thus those who remained to establish higher wage levels based on their rate of scarcity. Due to the decreased supply and increased demand for labor to work on agricultural land, many of the class reali-ties of the late medieval era shifted. The peasant class ultimately advanced the most in terms of quality of life, which helped to begin a rapid decline in serfdom as one of the prevailing models of economic activity. As John Gower, an English land overseer, complained in 1375:

> The world goeth fast from bad to worse, when shepherd and cowherd . . . demand more for their labor than the masterbaliff was wont to take in days gone by. Labor is now at so high a price that he who will order his business aright must pay five or six shillings now for what cost him two in former times. . . . Ha! . . . The poor and small folk . . . demand to be fed better than their masters. (Friedrich 1986, 135)

In addition to a decline in the labor pool, Europe experienced a decline in the prices of various commodities. Before to the 1340s the price of wheat throughout Europe was high, primarily because of the overpopulation in many communities prior to the plague, as well as varied crop yields. However, due to a number of factors, including the drop in the number of potential consumers because of the thinning of the plague-ridden population, the price of wheat underwent a major reduction. Ultimately, this change in the price of wheat forced some landowners to develop new labor-saving devices that could assist in maximizing crop yields, largely through the development of more efficient tools to help with cultivation of the fields.

Finally, the arena of economic output was dramatically enhanced as labor shortages forced the development of innovative approaches to achieving goals with smaller labor forces. Historian David Herlihy points to the invention of Johann Gutenberg's printing press in 1453, which came to replace the teams of monastic copyists who were diminished by the plague in higher numbers than the larger population due to their close living quarters. Other innovations of the time were new designs for ships that could ultimately take much smaller crews on longer journeys, and weaponry that was far more efficient in battle than were armies made up only of large numbers of soldiers (Herlihy 1997, 50). Such innovations coincided with the beginning of an era of European exploration and conquest and provide some understanding of factors that enabled the period of rapid exploration and discovery that evolved from the late 1400s onward.

Plague of 1600s: Emergence of New Thinking in Science, Governance, and Medicine

The early to mid-1600s was a period of major political and social transition in England. By the middle of the 1600s, the nation had experienced several cycles of the plague. Each brought a shift in thought processes in one form or another. After the plague of 1603, for example, Francis Bacon wrote *The Advancement of Learning*, which called for a reexamination of various approaches to obtaining knowledge. The older ways of thinking about scientific processes, Bacon felt, brought humankind no closer to identifying a means to deal with the plague. Prior to this work, the notion of learning meant repetitive studying and being able to largely recite many of the classic works by ancient philosophers. Bacon, however, argued for learning based on empiricism. Such a process facilitated new approaches to observation and experiment, and ultimately led to new ways of thinking about and building knowledge.

In addition to *The Advancement of Learning*, Bacon's *Novum Organum* and *New Atlantis* later served as an inspiration to some of England's best scientific minds in the mid-1600s, including Christopher Wren, Robert Boyle, and John Wilkins. These three thinkers established a society in 1660 to explore some of the more pressing scientific questions of the era, using mechanisms of empiricism as outlined by Bacon. Through their work, they were able to obtain support from King Charles II for their new society, get their organization written into the 1663 Royal Charter, and have it officially renamed the "Royal Society."

Since its founding, the Royal Society has served as an institution that promotes scientific exploration. It aided in the development of intellectual perceptions that would provide new ways of thinking about science and continue to shape how society would develop. In some cases, the seeds of doubt that raced through European intellectual communities, partially as a result of the challenges presented by the plague, would shape societal thought and response to later confrontations with the plague and other diseases.

By the middle of the century, a new cycle of plague served to leverage further stages of advancement in science that would be linked to the advances of the Royal Society. In April 1665, news of a new outbreak of the plague spreading in London reached much of the country. Having already suffered through several cycles of the disease, people in urban centers such as London knew that if one had the resources to do so, it was better to flee to the countryside and other less populated areas than to confront the plague. Thus, thousands of people found themselves headed into semi-isolation where they would await news from the more populated cities that the plague had subsided.

One person who found himself in isolation during this period, waiting for news of the demise of this plague cycle, was a student at Trinity College in Cambridge by the name of Isaac Newton. Like other students in 1665, Newton left his formal studies to wait out the plague. For Newton, however, this year of a near solitary existence enabled him to advance his study of mathematics far more than many of his peers, and ultimately to reach some of his conclusions about the operations of science principles. He would begin to articulate them in notes that would lead to the development of his *Philosophiæ Naturalis Principia Mathematica,* also known as *The Principia.*

The Principia presented Newton's laws of motion and his law of universal gravitation, which would influence generations of thinkers. By the 1700s this writing would influence Enlightenment-era authors such as Adam Smith, Montesquieu, and Voltaire, all of whom would further the process of applying scientific principles to some of the pressing challenges of government and society.

England's plague of the 1600s would also shape thinking in the area of medicine, helping to move medical theory and practice into new areas that were further distanced from Galenist thought. In England, four categories of individuals who practiced the field of medicine emerged. First were the traditional physicians. These practitioners were the most beholden to many of the Galenistic approaches, still adhering to the notion that balancing humors was the best way to address any ailments that people might encounter. Because the physicians were often viewed as the most competent, they were also the costliest of the practitioners. Second were the apothecaries, who were grounded in prescribing various medicines that would help to cure a sickness. Third were surgeon barbers, who performed various surgical procedures to address ailments. Finally, there were people who engaged in informal medical practices, sometimes based on folklore or traditions passed down generations.

Because the physician's services were costlier, and often catered to the population that was the first to flee the cities during the plague, many of these practitioners also left the cities at such times. As a result, in 1665 the people living in London and other cities found themselves with fewer physicians and more of the other categories of practitioners to call upon to help them confront the plague and other illnesses. For the apothecaries in particular, this provided an opportunity to advance the legitimacy of their practice and help to position this alternative to Galenistic approaches to medicine. Their belief in the development and prescription of medicines helped to advance what would ultimately become pharmaceutical approaches for handling illnesses.

In time, new approaches to inquiry also led to knowledge about the human body and the development of medical techniques that blended methods from the physicians, apothecaries, and surgeons. In attempts to understand how to prevent the plague, new pathways began to develop which in most cases had no affect on the plague's appearance but did advance thinking about possible curative processes that ultimately benefited medical science as a whole. Anatomical investigations, which began in earlier plague cycles, were now pursued with a greater sense of urgency. The fields of medical science experienced the social impetus to begin a transition that would continue in the following decades.

THE PLAGUE: 1700s

By the early 1700s, communities throughout Europe had become accustomed to the plague. It had already swept through the continent on several occasions—never, though, in as such a forceful wave as did the plague of the 1340s. With news of each new wave's arrival, local officials would identify ways to prepare their communities. Notions such as prevention and preparation were increasingly finding their ways into the thinking of public officials.

In 1720, a French trading ship known as *Le Grand Saint Antoine* sailed into the French port at Marseilles. Aboard the ship were several sailors who had been stricken by the plague, yet were able to make it past the quarantine established by the city. In little time, the infection spread to all sections of the city, and by the end of June, most medical specialists agreed that a plague outbreak had arrived in Marseilles.

Marseilles was rapidly quarantined from the rest of France and much of the rest of Europe. The provincial government noted that individuals hoping to go into or out of Marseilles would be punished with death. Other governments across Europe reacted with their own systems of quarantine and other policy approaches. In England, Parliament reacted in two distinct ways that signified a transition in plague defense strategies. Unlike past efforts, which had focused on curing those stricken by the plague, the methods assumed in the 1720s aimed to develop rapid and effective means of ensuring prevention.

In London, Parliament commissioned Doctor Richard Meade to develop a plan for responding to the plague outbreak in Marseilles and limiting its potential impact in England. Meade's perspectives built upon the work of Girolamo Fracastoro, who in the 1500s wrote *On Contagion and Contagious Disease and Their Cure,* which suggested that contagious disease is transmitted by self-multiplying "seeds." Based on this theory drawn from Fracastoro's work, Meade drew up a statement on prevention of the plague entitled *A Short Discourse Concerning Pestilential Contagion and The Methods to Be Used to Prevent It,* which argued that the proper approach to preventing the spread of disease was to minimize the opportunities for the contagions to spread. Such a viewpoint nearly replaced the Galenistic perspective that disease was caused by bad vapors and their impact on the balance of humors, shifting the emphasis in response to the plague from cure to prevention.

Meade's publication ran through several editions during its first year and ultimately led to the House of Lords appointing a committee to inspect the laws enforced against the plague in order to consider the proper means of preventing the arrival of the infection. In late January 1721, the House of Lords passed a bill that contained many strict provisions for limiting the plague's entrance into Britain. It demanded the maintenance of a close quarantine for all vessels coming from infected ports and levied a strict penalty for concealing the fact that a given vessel had come from an infected location or had plague-stricken persons on board. In October, the king commented on the necessity of preventing the spread of the infection to England, and not long afterward, an act was passed to enable the king to prohibit commercial trade with any country that was, or was anticipated to be, infected with the plague.

CONCLUSION

To date, the plague that ravaged Europe from the 1300s to the 1700s exists as one of the worst medical crises to confront humankind. Its impact on societies had both immediate and long-term consequences, particularly on the evolution of thought in a broader context. Many of the changes leveraged advances for the future of medicine, as well as new developments in societal progress.

Two frameworks might be used to consider the waves of plague that ravaged Europe during those four hundred years. The first is through the lens of the crisis of the time—recognizing that during its first major cycle, the plague was responsible for the deaths of over a third of Europeans within a period of less than two years. Communities had to adapt to the wide-scale shock as well as to the population declines that came with the plague as it cycled through Europe during this era. Elements of societal adaptation in light of such challenges were crucial for understanding the response to this crisis.

The second framework recognizes many of the changes within European societies and that, in turn, helped to give rise to perspectives and institutions that shaped much of the modern era. It is from this framework that we might understand the impact of the plague on advances that would surface in the medical world, as well as in the fields of science, government, and other societal realms.

Many of these advances stemmed from the differences that people saw in their ability to determine their own fate. Notions of human determinism, and not divine intervention, became critical to the experiences of people in Europe and elsewhere. While people continued to believe that God played a central role in what happened to humankind, they were also beginning to accept the idea that their own actions affected what happened to them.

If it were not for many of the societal changes forced by the plagues that came in the late Middle Ages, many of the perspectives of the Enlightenment would not have emerged. The Enlightenment provided much of the thinking that would begin to develop in the early years of the early-modern era. Advances in the areas of self-determination and the sciences were driven, to a degree, by some of the critical developments and challenges of the era of the Enlightenment. Many of these developments were framed as people began to further challenge the norms of a society that had to adapt to various elements of the plague era.

Ultimately, these changes provided greater access to the institutions of knowledge production, as well as the scientific foundations, and gave the confidence in scientific processes that would lead to further medical progress, as well as advances in the use of science and deterministic frameworks in other areas of human political, social, and economic life. It was these advances that began to bring humankind increasingly into the modern era, face to face with many of the challenges that would be both of our own making and a product of our evolving interactions with nature.

5

Germ Theory, Cholera, and Infectious Disease

It would be easy to reach a consensus that the room where a sailor by the name of John Harnold stayed at Number 8, New Lane, would be a poor choice for later guests. In the early fall of 1848, after arriving in London on a ship known as the *Elbe*, Mr. Harnold checked into his room. Either before arriving, or perhaps even while in the lodging house, Harnold ingested a small dose of bacteria. These bacteria did what they, as well as the trillions of other microorganisms, instinctually do—they sought to reproduce. In the particular case of the *Vibrio cholerae* bacteria that Harnold ingested, the ideal place of reproduction was in his small intestine, through a process that can happen only if the bacteria injects a toxin into the cells of the host's intestine. As a result of both the toxin and the overall process of bacterial replication, Harnold's ability to absorb water was greatly reduced. Like other victims of cholera, the disease that occurs as *Vibrio cholerae* bacteria follow this course of activity, Harnold would have most likely expelled water in great quantities through continuous vomiting and diarrhea and suffered from resulting dehydration. If his encounter with the *Vibrio cholerae* bacteria was similar to that of other cholera victims, John Harnold would have been dead within a matter of hours.

Harnold's battle with cholera was an example of one of the thousands of cholera victims in England in the nineteenth century. The outbreaks that occurred in several regions of the country led to an evolving understanding of both public health and the rapidly emerging fields of bacteriology. New practices in the areas of epidemiology and sanitation control and an emergent knowledge of germs as a cause of disease helped to form a growing sense of how epidemics—not only of cholera, but also of other infectious diseases—might be handled.

The London cholera epidemics came at the beginning of a period of increasing advances in the understanding of infectious diseases such as tuberculosis, typhoid, and rabies, which then would lead to the development of new approaches for handling the infections that would erupt in the next century and a half.

URBAN GROWTH AND SANITATION

At the center of London's microbe challenge was the problem of how to dispose of increasing amounts of human waste. Through the first half of the 1800s, London experienced tremendous growth in its urban population. In 1801, the city had slightly under a million people. Within fifty years, the population grew to over 2.3 million residents (George 2008, 26). With such rapid growth came a number of challenges. Where to house people? How to ensure that there would be enough jobs for them? How would enough food be secured to feed the population? And what should be done with the population's waste?

For years, human waste in London, as well as many other cities, was collected largely in cesspools located in or near the basements of people's homes. For much of the 1700s and early 1800s, the cesspools were emptied by night soil men, who in turn sold the waste to nearby farmlands where it would be used as fertilizer. While this job provided a semi-adequate living for many of the urban poor, it was vulnerable to various market forces. As London grew, the supply of urban night soil outgrew the demand at nearby farmlands. This problem of oversupply was compounded as it became cheaper to import guano, bird or bat excrement, perceived as a more productive and less offensive form of fertilizer. Finally, it became increasingly common for people in some of London's poorer communities not to pay the night soil collection fees. As a result, uncollected human waste built up in many areas. As one civil engineer noted:

> I found whole areas of the cellars of both houses were full of nightsoil to the depth of three feet, which had been permitted for years to ac-

cumulate from the overflows of the cesspools. . . . I would mention another case amongst many more in St. Giles's Parish. . . . Upon passing through the passage of the first house I found the yard covered in nightsoil, from the overflowing of the privy to the depth of nearly six inches and bricks were placed to enable the inmates to get across dry shod. (Johnson 2006, 10)

Many of the city's residents used several solutions for addressing waste buildup. First was the continuous use of cesspools and other waste depositories. Frequently, however, the solution for many was to simply dump much of the waste, particularly from the overflowing cesspools, into the Thames River, where some of it would decompose as the river made its way through London. In other cases, it ended up on the riverbanks. A letter published in the *Times of London* in 1855 depicted the result:

The smell was very bad, and common to the whole of the water; it was the same as that which now comes up from the gulley holes in the streets; the whole river was for the time a real sewer. Having just returned from out of the country air, I was, perhaps more affected by it than by others; but I do not think I could have gone on to Lamberth or Chelsea, and I was glad to enter the streets for an atmosphere which, except near the sink holes, I found much sweeter than that on the river. . . . If there be sufficient authority to remove a putrescent pond from the neighborhood of a few simple dwellings, surely the river which flows so many miles through London ought not to be allowed to become a fermenting sewer. (Faraday 1855, 284)

London's human waste problem was coupled with the challenge of securing an adequate water supply for its growing population base. In an era when the field of microbiology was still in its early stages, the full depth of the risk in using the same body of water for depositing waste and drawing water was not fully understood. As a result, the drinking water processed by five of the nine companies that used water from the Thames River for London's drinking water supply was far below standards that we might expect today. Few people at the time saw the potential links in the early and mid-1800s between drinking from a polluted source of water and the public health challenges confronting the city's residents.

One of the individuals who expressed concern was Edwin Chadwick, the English social reformer whose 1842 *Report on the Sanitary Conditions of the Labouring Population of Great Britain* noted the link between London's thousands of cesspools and the broader health challenges around the city. At the time Chadwick began his efforts, London had a system in place for parishes throughout the city to be responsible for administering to the needs of the poor. Excessive decentralization among the 16,000 parishes in London alone led to both inefficient provision of services and neglect within many of the districts. Recognizing the need for reform, Chadwick argued for the development of what ultimately became England's first sanitary commission. This commission set the foundation for future commissions both within England and elsewhere for further integration between public health services and strategies for addressing infectious disease.

Chadwick's work was part of a broader movement that was occurring in various nations, where practitioners in the areas of medicine were beginning to map the spread of diseases and links between diseases and broader sanitation needs.

LONDON'S CHOLERA OUTBREAKS

A decade and a half before John Harnold checked into the lodging house on New Lane, a researcher by the name of John Snow engaged in a series of studies examining the high incidence of cholera among miners in an area known as Killinkworth Court. Snow had noticed that miners in England were the most common victims of cholera, largely due to the condition in which many of the miners worked, spending sizable portions of the day in unsanitary spaces underground. As Snow observed:

> Pitmen are differently situated from every other class of workmen in many important particulars. There are no privies in the coal-pits, or as I believe, in other mines. The workmen stay so long in the mines that they are obliged to take a supply of food with them, which they eat invariably with unwashed hands, and without knife and fork. (Snow 1855, 19)

Coal miners were among the poorest of England's population at the time. Snow's broader observations on matters of poverty led him to draw various conclusions that linked poverty to the spread of cholera. Snow noted that the close living quarters of the poor often aided in the spread of the disease:

> It is amongst the poor, where a whole family lives, sleeps, cooks, eats, and washes in a single room, that cholera has been found to spread when once introduced, and still more in those places termed common lodging houses, in which several families were crowded into a single room. It was amongst the vagrant class, who lived in this crowded state, that cholera was most fatal in 1832. (Snow 1855, 18)

Snow's observations of the poor included correlations between lack of cleanliness and incidents of cholera. As he observed:

> Nothing has been found to favor the extension of cholera more than want of personal cleanliness, whether arising from habit or scarcity of water, although the circumstances till lately remained unexplained. The bed linen nearly always becomes wetted by the cholera evacuations, and as these are devoid of the usual colour and odour, the hands of the person waiting on the patient become soiled without their knowing it; and unless these persons are scrupulously cleanly in their habits, and wash their hands before taking food, they must accidentally swallow some of the excretion and leave some on the food they handle or prepare, which has to be eaten by the rest of the family who amongst the working classes, often have to take their meals in the sick room; hence the thousands of instances in which, amongst this class of the population, a case of cholera in one member of the family is followed by other cases; whilst medical men and others, who merely visit the patients, generally escape. The post mortem inspection of the bodies of cholera patients has hardly ever been followed by the disease that I am aware, this being a duty that is necessarily followed by careful washing of the hands; and it is not the habit of medical men to be taking food on such an occasion. On the other hand, the duties performed about the bodies, such as laying it out, when done by women of the working class, who make the occasion one of eating and drinking, are often followed by an attack of cholera; and persons who merely attend the funeral, and have no connection with the body, frequently contract the disease, in consequence, apparently, of partaking of food which has been prepared or handled by those having duties about the cholera patient, or his linen and bedding. (Snow 1855, 16)

When examined from a class perspective, cholera, particularly as it appeared in urban settings, began to provide a bit of a puzzle for public health workers who were beginning to explore the impact in further detail. In contrast to explaining the presence of cholera in families from impoverished backgrounds, identifying how such conditions could surface in wealthier families was a different challenge for Snow. Several observations of water transmission led him to the conclusion that, ultimately, it was through water that cholera was being spread. Snow began to notice that cesspools occasionally overflowed into wells where people retrieved their water for drinking and other household needs.

> When on the other hand, cholera is introduced into the better kind of houses, as it often is, by means that will be afterwards pointed out, it hardly ever spreads from one member of the family to another. The constant use of the hand basin and towel, and the fact of the apartments for cooking and eating being distinct from the sick room are the cause of this. (Snow 1855, 18)

Snow's observations on potential causes of cholera's spread during the 1830s were of particular use when England experienced a second wave of cholera in the late 1840s. During this epidemic, 14,000 people died in London alone and 50,000 people died across the country. It was in this period that Snow continued to draw connections between cholera and the water systems, arguing that the practice of flushing sewers into the river made the 1849 epidemic worse. Within less than a decade, he would have a greater opportunity to explore his hypothesis on the spread of cholera through water systems.

THE SOHO OUTBREAK

On the night of August 31, 1854, six years after John Harnold's ill-fated stay in London, there was a sudden outbreak of cholera in London's Soho section. Within ten days of the outbreak, cholera had claimed 500 fatalities within 300 yards of the intersection of Cambridge and Broad Streets in the center of the community. Within two weeks, nearly 750 people living within

250 yards of the Cambridge and Broad intersection had died (Johnson 2006, 160).

Snow observed that high incidences of cholera were occurring among persons drawing water from a well on Broad Street that Snow had noted was critical. Further investigation revealed that a sewer passed close to the well. Ultimately, by mapping where the deaths occurred, Snow concluded that the water pump at Broad Street was a critical link in the spread of cholera.

> It must be obvious that there are various ways in which the deceased persons may have taken it without the knowledge of their friends. The water was used for mixing with spirits in all the public houses around. It was used likewise at dining-rooms and coffee-shops. The keeper of a coffee-shop in the neighborhood, which was frequented by mechanics, and where the pump water was supplied at dinner time, informed me (on 6th September) that she was already aware of nine of her customers who were dead. The pump water was also sold in various little shops, with a teaspoon of powder in it under the name of sherbert; and it may have been distributed in various other ways with which I am unacquainted. The pump was frequented much more than is usual, even for a London pump in a populous neighborhood. (Snow 1855, 42)

Snow's work provides a depiction of the means by which cholera is spread between various communities. Also it is known for the level of detail demonstrated in tracking down the emergence of various outbreaks. His work in tracing the spread of cholera also underscored an emerging belief that cholera was the product of some form of infectious agent that was being spread between people.

Coupled with Chadwick's contribution, Snow's efforts were part of a broader movement occurring in the mid- to late 1800s as officials working in medicine and government were becoming increasingly concerned about the spread of new disease outbreaks such as cholera. As patterns of industrialization progressed, officials were becoming aware of the public health challenges that they would need to confront as the world slowly became urbanized, interconnected, and aware of the roles of microorganisms in the state of our health.

CHAPTER 5

Conclusion: Germ Theory and the Legacy of the London Cholera Epidemic

The scientific advances leading to germ theory in the mid-1800s helped us to develop our comprehension of how infectious disease spreads. The shift, particularly driven by the work influenced by early bacteriologists such as Henle and Pasteur, ultimately framed the means for responding to many of the infectious diseases that had haunted humankind for all of our existence. These discoveries would also prove critical as we wrestled with future public health crises. Coupled with the world of epidemiologists and public health planners such as Chadwick and Snow, cities and nations were finding a number of important patterns related to the spread of cholera and other infectious diseases.

The advances in microbiology provided a basis for asking questions about the spread of disease to a far greater extent than people had experienced before. Much of this newfound knowledge would provide critical information in the early years of the twentieth century as doctors and scientists wrestled with a number of pressing challenges to ensuring the overall health of the public.

In addition to advances in the world of microbiology, there were improvements in the relations between nations that would stem from the challenges presented by cholera. In 1851, several nations convened a meeting of representatives from governments to explore combined strategies for addressing cholera, which had by then become a concern throughout Europe. The meeting developed an international framework for matters of sanitation and a series of strategies for implementation across nations to address cholera and other health concerns.

In time, these efforts would provide an important foundation for a series of treaties and new institutions that ultimately addressed health concerns on a global scale. Before each mechanism could be fully set in place, the world would encounter a few additional major health crises, one of which would derive from what is normally considered a common health nuisance—the flu.

72

6

Infectious Disease and Nascent Public Health Infrastructures
The 1918 Influenza Epidemic

In March 1918, the chief medical officer of the Eighty-Ninth Division at Camp Funston, Kansas, sent a telegram to the Surgeon General's Office in Washington, DC. "Virulent secondary streptococcic pneumonia following epidemic pseudo influenza present," began the telegram. "Many deaths influenza following immediately two extremely severe dust storms" (Byerly 2005, 70). The officer asked the surgeon general to send out an inspector to investigate the outbreak.

There would be scores of victims of the flu at Camp Funston that spring. Other military bases would also find themselves battling with flu outbreaks. For medical practitioners, the high presence of flu on bases was puzzling. Bases were full of young soldiers, who under normal circumstances would have immune systems strong enough to fight major infections. This flu, however, was different.

The 1918 flu provides numerous lessons for examining the spread of infectious disease for both the remainder of the twentieth century and the early twenty-first. Globally, over 20 million people would die from the flu in less than a year. In the United States, more than 675,000 people died within a matter of months. As a result, numerous questions arose regarding the role of public health systems and the response of the scientific community in finding a means for addressing this illness, and the impact of the 1918 flu on the evolution of public health systems in the years following.

Three critical backdrops are important for considering the flu of 1918. First was the emergence of a growing urban public health infrastructure in the United States. The existence of the citywide public health systems established a tension with one of the other institutions gaining stature at the time, the U.S. Public Health Service. This institution was critical in a debate that would surface repeatedly as strategies for health concerns were explored for the rest of the century. What were the roles of central health agencies in a national medical infrastructure that had historically been decentralized?

Second was the backdrop of World War I. Thousands of troops were being moved from one nation to another, many of them transported in tightly packed ships across the Atlantic Ocean between Europe and the United States. When they reached the battlefields, many of these same soldiers confronted the new weaponry of toxic gases that was being integrated into warfare, and as they wrestled with the exhaustion of life on the battlefronts of Europe, both their exhaustion and their exposure to toxins made them increasingly susceptible to the flu virus. This susceptibility plus the movement of troops contributed to the flu's transmission between countries and continents.

Third, the outbreak occurred as the United States was completing its transition from being primarily rural to a predominantly urban nation. New urban centers provided ample opportunities for the spread of the flu from the infected to the uninfected. The commission of public health officials battling the flu in cities provided ample opportunities to consider strategies for containing the spread of infectious diseases such as the 1918 influenza. The combination of these factors provided a framework for asking if our social patterns create an enhanced risk in the spread of infections.

PUBLIC HEALTH INFRASTRUCTURE

Struggles with infectious disease throughout the 1800s left much of the United States with public systems of varying degrees of efficiency. Much of this local infrastructure emerged from a belief that the provision of medical services should occur at a local level and not be driven by a national institution. The U.S. Constitution places the responsibility for public health issues in the hands of the states, not the federal government, which has raised an abundance of questions regarding the role of the federal and the state governments in addressing these issues.

Any national infrastructure that existed was based in the U.S. Public Health Service, a direct descendent of the Marine Hospital Service, established under the presidency of John Adams. The Marine Hospital Service was set up in 1789 when the federal government provided hospital facilities for the merchant marines. In the 1870s the service established a commissioned corps of medical officers who began to extend their role beyond the care of sailors alone to providing support to communities during periods of public health crisis. Gradually the commissioned corps expanded in numbers and began to function as a federal agency that could be called upon by any city or state health authority during such crises.

By the early 1900s, the duties of the Marine Hospital Corps had became so extensive that in 1902 it was renamed the Public Health and Marine Hospital Service. The service was controlled by the secretary of the treasury, who, along with the service's director, the surgeon general, determined policy. Serving as surgeon general was Rupert Blue, who had made a name for himself in the bubonic plague and typhoid outbreaks in San Francisco in the aftermath of the 1906 earthquake.

SPRING AND EARLY SUMMER 1918: BACKGROUND OF WAR

We now know that influenza, like many other viruses, normally will infect people who have not had some exposure to it. Those who have been exposed, and survive, often build up a resistance that makes it difficult to be infected by the same strain twice. If there are no more susceptible members of a population, the virus often will burn out or change into a different and sometimes more virulent strain. Following this viral pattern, by the late spring and summer of 1918, the incidents of flu began to decline at Funston and other bases in the United States, as the flu virus increasingly ran out of a population to which it could spread. At the same time as the flu's presence in the United States was diminishing, however, reports of outbreaks began to surface throughout Europe.

At first, many of the European outbreaks were limited to military bases and troops. In a short time, however, the flu spread from military forces to Europe's civilian populations. In London, there were over 700 deaths from the flu during July 1918. Hamburg lost 214 of its residents to the flu. In Switzerland over 50,000 cases of the flu were reported in July (Crosby 1976, 28). In Spain, between May and June, roughly eight million people caught the flu.

Aside from its spread in the United States and Europe, the 1918 flu infected other parts of the world. Much of the impact was seen in nations with port cities that received sailors carrying the flu. Sierra Leone, for example was one of the most affected countries in Africa. In August 1918, the capital of Freetown received the British ship HMS *Mantua*. Aboard the ship were 200 sailors who, during their journey had been infected by the flu. Within weeks of the arrival of the *Mantua*, the flu spread throughout Sierra Leone, ultimately infecting two-thirds of the people and killing 3 percent of the country's entire population.

This flu had quickly become a global problem.

LATE SUMMER AND FALL 1918: THE URBAN SPREAD

As the summer progressed, public officials in the United States began receiving reports of the flu's impact throughout Europe, and anticipated that if it were to resurface in the United States, the flu would be devastating. Thus, when Rupert Blue began receiving numerous reports on the flu in Europe, he began to forecast that in the relatively near future, he would need to prepare the nation for the arrival of a much more powerful wave of the flu than had been encountered the previous spring. Blue's powers as surgeon general were limited, however, as he developed possible responses to the anticipated return of a more virulent strain. While Blue could request that medical officers remain aware of cases of influenza, he did not have the authority to quarantine. He merely could monitor and keep people apprised of outbreaks as they occurred. His lack of power represented one of the primary challenges at the time—the roles that a national authority could undertake to address public health concerns were limited.

Aware that the soldiers in Europe would be returning to highly populated port cities in the United States, and that many of the soldiers would likely be infected with the flu, Blue did basically all that he could and ordered that medical officers in port cities who oversaw quarantine stations remain alert for any cases of influenza on vessels arriving from Europe.

As the disembarkation point for many of the ships carrying soldiers who had been on the European battlefront, Boston was a major port of concern for Blue and other health officials. If there was to be a new outbreak stemming from the virulent strain that had been appearing in Europe during the latter months of the war, then certainly Boston, they felt, would be a target.

On August 27, 1918, two soldiers in Boston who had recently returned from Europe were stricken with influenza. Two days later, fifty-eight cases were reported in the city. Within two weeks, two thousand men in the First Naval District in Boston were battling the flu. By early September, reports of the virus were spreading to both the civilian population and other military bases near Boston. The fears expressed by Surgeon General Blue were being realized. The flu had arrived at a major port in the United States. Within weeks, it had spread from the naval population to the civilian population. By September, an estimated 85,000 citizens in Massachusetts had contracted influenza. Seven hundred people died of flu and pneumonia in the last week of the month (Crosby 1976, 53).

Thirty miles to the west of Boston was Camp Devens, one of Rupert Blue's other concerns. Camp Devens was originally built to hold 35,000 soldiers. Due to the war needs, the camp was filled beyond capacity, to the point of holding 45,000 soldiers, 5,000 of them under canvas coverage. On the seventh day of September, a soldier from Company B at Camp Devens reported to the infirmary with influenza. The next day, one dozen soldiers reported to the infirmary ill. Within two weeks, this number had grown to over 6,000 men stationed at the camp. Devens, like Boston, was experiencing a wave of flu victims.

By the end of the month, there reportedly had been more than 14,000 cases of influenza. Over 750 of the cases proved fatal. A letter from a doctor at Camp Devens described the situation:

> These men start with what appears to be an attack of la grippe or influenza, and when brought to the hospital they very rapidly develop the most vicious type of pneumonia that has ever been seen. Two hours after admission they have the mahogany spots over the cheek bones, and few hours later you can begin to see the cyanosis extending from their ears and spreading all over the face, until it is hard to distinguish the coloured men from the white. It is only a few hours then until death comes, and it is simply a struggle for air until they suffocate. It is horrible. One can stand it to see one, two or twenty men die, but to see these poor devils dropping like flies sort of gets on your nerves. We have been averaging about 100 deaths per day, and still keep it up. There is no doubt in my mind that there is a new mixed infection here, but what I don't know. (A Letter from Camp Devins [sic], Mass. 1918)

While Boston and Camp Devens were of concern, another city being monitored closely for flu outbreaks was New York. Driving much of the concern was the reality that New York had thousands of people living in the city's tenements. These dwellings were known for being overcrowded, poorly ventilated, and an ideal ground for the spread of disease.

New York, however, benefited from a public health system that had proved itself as being able to respond to the unique health challenges that arose in the city. A few years earlier, for example, New York waged a battle with typhoid that ultimately forced the city to enhance its infrastructure for responding to infectious diseases.

Coupled with many of the Progressive era municipal reforms that were being tested in the city, New York had in place a number of systems that its public health officials anticipated would assist in preventing the spread of infectious diseases.

On September 18, 1918, the Board of Health made influenza a reportable disease in New York City. Throughout the city, district centers were opened to address the health concerns and provide services through a community-based network of nurses and other trained personnel. Many of these individuals served as critical frontline workers as communities struggled with how they would respond to the pressing short-term needs related to the flu.

New York assumed an approach that was unique among cities at the time. While the health commissioners of most cities, with the support of city councils and state governments, were closing many of the public facilities, New York opted to keep the majority of its facilities open. While various precautions were taken, New York's health commissioner explained why he was acting contrary to actions pursued in other settings. As he said in a *New York Times* interview:

> I do know the conditions of New York, and I know that in our city one of the most important methods of disease control is in the public school system. . . . We have practically 1,000,000 children in the public schools, about 750,000 of them from tenement homes. These homes are frequently unsanitary and crowded. The children's parents are occupied with the manifold duties involved in keeping the wolf from the door. No matter how loving they may be—and of course, they are just as loving as any parents anywhere—they simply have not the time to give the necessary attention to the initial symptoms of disease, even if they should have enough knowledge to recognize and meet them, which they rarely have. . . . When children are sent to school they go away from home with clean faces and hands and with clean outer clothing, at least. They leave their often unsanitary homes for large, clean, airy school buildings, where there is always a system of inspection and examination enforced, and where during the epidemic all the details of such work were rightly adhered to. ("Epidemic Lessons" 1918)

The approach outlined by the health commissioner may have had mixed results. While New York was not as heavily stricken by the flu, proportionally to other cities, there were indications that the city did nonetheless face some severe challenges from the flu.

Within a few short months, for example, it had become evident that the challenges of the flu in New York would stretch into many areas providing social services. For instance, the New York Health Commission reported that 21,000 children had been made half or full orphans by the influenza epidemic. In 7,200 families, either one parent or both had died. Of these families, about 700 would need assistance from the city, the commission noted, and about 2,000 children would be affected and in need of aid.

South of New York, the *Philadelphia Inquirer*'s September 19, 1918, edition published a headline that spoke to the impending challenge that Philadelphia would face as it confronted the flu: "Spanish Influenza Sends 600 Sailors to Hospital Here—No Concern Felt." While the number of sailors infected was a certain sign that the flu had come to Philadelphia, the city's bureau of health indicated minimal concern about the spread of the flu beyond the military communities and into the general communities of citizens.

The network of medical institutions that was established early in Philadelphia's history provides a frame for understanding how the 1918 flu impacted the city. Philadelphia had long prided itself on such institutions such as the medical programs at the University of Pennsylvania and Hahnemann Hospital. Also, the city had wrestled with previous instances of medical crisis, the most famous of which was the yellow fever epidemic of the late 1700s, which helped to establish a public health infrastructure for responding to the challenges of a major infectious outbreak.

Philadelphia faced the challenge of being located near several military bases. Thus, as troops returned stateside carrying the flu, they often served as vectors for the flu into new areas. As home to one of the major naval yards on the East Coast and only a short distance from Fort Dix in New Jersey and Fort Meade in Maryland, the city would certainly see an influx of military personnel returning from Europe at the end of the war.

Despite the outbreak of the flu in Philadelphia, public officials decided to proceed with a major event that would bring thousands of people into close proximity with one another. Throughout the nation, Liberty Loan parades were being used as opportunities to promote bond purchases to help finance the war. Philadelphia, like many cities, was due to host one of the parades. Officials had to weigh the question of whether to proceed with the plans for the parade, despite the presence of the flu. Ultimately, they decided to move forward with it. On September 28, over two hundred thousand people gathered to view the Fourth Liberty Loan Drive Parade, which stretched twenty-three city blocks through the streets of the city and provided an opportunity for the influenza virus to spread among thousands of potential victims.

Within days of the parade, the city exploded with an outbreak of the flu. On October 1, over 630 new civilian cases of flu were reported. Eight days later, over 4,000 cases were reported. During the second week of October, 2,600 Philadelphians died of pneumonia or influenza, and during the third week of October, an additional 9,500 Philadelphians died.

One of the pressing challenges that Philadelphia encountered in this outbreak was the limited number of medical professionals who were available to assist in handling the upsurge in influenza victims. Many of the city's doctors and nurses were in Europe providing support for war-related medical needs there. In many cases, the city had to rely on students still in training to be medical professionals. Medical doctor Isaac Starr, who at the time was just starting his third year at the University of Pennsylvania School of Medicine, recalled the situation:

> Soon the beds were full, but nobody on my floor was very ill. The patients had fever but little else. Many seemed to have sought admission chiefly because everybody in the family was sick and no one was left at home who could take care of them. . . . Unhappily the clinical features of many soon changed drastically. As their lungs filled with rales and the patients became short of breath and increasingly cyanotic. After gasping for several hours they became delirious and incontinent. And many died struggling to clear their airways of a blood tinged froth that sometimes gushed form their nose and mouth. It was a dreadful business. (Sachs 2007)

Other medical professionals recollected the impact of the flu on patients with whom they worked, including this excerpt from the annual report for the Visiting Nurse Society in 1918:

> . . . in a tragic case, the nurse arrived to find the mother of a family ill with a temperature of 105. In the next room lay the father, who had been dead for twenty-four hours. In the parlor was a little child huddled on the sofa with a temperature of 105. The two other children were well. No doctor had been to that family. The nurse gave emergency treatment

at once to the woman and sent an urgent call to the police station for a doctor. After much difficulty, a doctor was procured, but the woman was already dying. However, the nurse was able to get a priest for her before she died. (Sharrar, Bogucki, and Uffelman n.d.)

A major challenge for Philadelphia was wrestling with providing various services generally needed by a population but that were significantly increased by the reality of the widespread flu. The city's primary morgue, which had a normal capacity for thirty-six bodies, had several hundred bodies, in some cases piled upon one another. Ultimately, the city had to acquire several supplemental morgues to deal with the additional bodies.

Philadelphia also clearly provided lessons for other cities regarding what not to do during an infectious breakout. The city had numerous warnings of the challenges of the influenza of 1918, but it chose to ignore the situations in Boston, New York, and other cities. A prime example was the decision to carry on with the Liberty Loan Parade and its resulting role in spreading the flu in Philadelphia. The city's minimal medical infrastructure (because most of its medical practitioners were in war-torn Europe) also severely challenged the city's response to the influenza crisis.

CONCLUSIONS

The mystery of the 1918 flu's appearance is matched by the mystery of its disappearance. Like the flu's disappearance from the United States in the spring of 1918, in the late fall of 1919, after leaving communities drastically altered across the nation, the influenza virus simply ran out of new nonimmune victims to attack.

The experience of the 1918 flu provided several lessons for later experiences of infectious disease. First was the need to develop an infrastructure to address new public health challenges. In the case of the flu, we witnessed both the response of local infrastructures and the development of a national infrastructure to help coordinate efforts to handle the challenges of the flu.

It also showed how faster transportation between regions would increase the spread of an infectious disease. Clearly one of the difficulties that surfaced with the flu was that troop movement caused people to move between cities, and later between nations, to a much greater extent and at much faster rates than ever before. Thus tracking the movements of the flu would be critical as health practitioners contemplated strategies to combat infectious diseases in the future.

Finally, the underlying tension of the roles of agencies at the local and national levels in addressing health issues was a critical concern that would increase over the next century as other infectious diseases loomed and questions arose regarding agency jurisdiction to develop and enforce strategies to mitigate future public health crises.

7

Twentieth-Century Optimism

In late December 1940, Albert Alexander, a forty-three-year-old British policeman, was admitted to Oxford's Radcliffe Infirmary. A few weeks before, Mr. Alexander had accidentally scratched himself by bumping into a rosebush near his home. The scratch became infected, and the site of the infection was deteriorating rapidly—ultimately leading to the appearance of abscesses all over Alexander's face. Despite initial efforts to cure him, his condition quickly grew worse; his fever continued, and the infection spread. By early February, it had reached his lungs and one of his eyes, which doctors subsequently removed.

In mid-February, Alexander's doctor gave him several injections of partially purified penicillin in an attempt to alleviate the infection. Within days, Alexander's temperature dropped and he could eat the meals that were given to him. Slowly, his condition improved, until the infirmary ran out of its limited supply of penicillin, at which point his condition rapidly declined. Within a month, he was dead.

Alexander's visit to the infirmary, and his brief moments of improvement, occurred slightly over twelve years after a biologist by the name of Alexander Fleming made an inadvertent discovery that would impact Albert Alexander's life and the lives of millions of other people. While on vacation in 1928, Dr. Fleming mistakenly left out a petri dish with bacteria. Upon returning to his lab, he noticed that one of the cultures of bacteria had been destroyed by a mold that had appeared in the dish. Fleming was able to isolate from the mold a liquid that killed many forms of bacteria—including those that caused some diseases.

During World War II, Fleming's discovery, by then known as penicillin, went into mass production as a means of battling infectious diseases that soldiers encountered. In time, penicillin became a critical tool in the battles against various infections for civilians as well. Many people saw it as a wonder drug that could fight a number of infections. In a broad sense, penicillin represented for many people a belief that through scientific advances we could defeat a number of infectious diseases.

The increasing popularity of Fleming's discovery came at a time when an institutional infrastructure continued to develop to address many of the pressing public health issues that concerned the global health community. Institutions such as the Centers for Disease Control and Prevention and the World Health Organization were critical components of this infrastructure. They contributed to a period of optimism in addressing public health crises, particularly in the fights against infectious diseases.

This chapter examines this period of medical optimism, which was largely based on institutional infrastructure and scientific progress that would advance many of the medical developments that were critical in minimizing the risks of infectious disease epidemics. I continue with an examination of the challenges of polio, smallpox, and malaria—three infectious diseases that were targeted for eradication during the latter half of the twentieth century. The strategies aimed at eliminating these diseases display the advances in science and medicine of the time, boosting the confidence of those working in and with international and domestic public health institutions as well as in the nongovernmental sector. For many policy makers, these advances supported a declaration that we had reached a time when we could proclaim that the age of infectious disease was over. This assumption is briefly examined along with the perspectives of those who challenge it.

MEDICAL HUBRIS AND THE LAUNCH OF THREE CAMPAIGNS: POLIO, SMALLPOX, AND MALARIA

By the middle of the twentieth century, a number of medical institutions that had established themselves as reputable and scientifically sound began identifying strategies for the eradication of infectious diseases, which were of pressing concern to public health workers and the community at large.

POLIO

In August 1921, a group of boy scouts in New York challenged a thirty-nine-year-old local hero by the name of Franklin Roosevelt to a race. The route chosen for the race involved a run across several yards followed by a swim across one of the nearby lakes. Shortly after returning to his family from the race with the boys, Roosevelt began to complain of not feeling well and retired early. The next morning he awoke with a high fever and severe numbness in one of his legs. By the end of the week he had lost all movement below his waist. William Keen, the doctor who quickly went to the Roosevelt home after he was called, recognized from the symptoms that Franklin Roosevelt had been stricken with polio. For the rest of his life, the polio that Franklin Roosevelt contracted would keep him limited to a wheelchair or able to walk only with some form of assistance.

While he was older than most victims of polio at the time, Roosevelt's contracting the disease was by no means a unique phenomenon. Polio had been known for years as a debilitating affliction in both the United States and other nations. For much of its history polio was believed to be a disease that struck in isolated situations. Now, however, large numbers of people were getting it.

Polio is spread when contaminated substances are swallowed—water from a swimming pool or a lake, for example. The virus invades the cells of the intestine and multiplies rapidly. The vast majority of polio infections remain in the gut and cause no serious problems. Occasionally, though, the virus makes its way from the digestive tract into the nervous system, where it begins killing off neurons. When this happens, as occurred to Roosevelt, paralysis is frequently the outcome.

In the first half of the twentieth century, polio was viewed as a major threat throughout the United States. In 1916, it became a disease of epidemic proportions, killing 6,000 people and leaving 27,000 people paralyzed. For the next several decades, the number of people infected with polio would continue to grow. By the early 1940s and 1950s, it was crippling an average of 35,000 people each year. The fear of the disease heightened as polio cases continued to rise. In 1952, polio reached its highest toll with more than 57,000 new cases reported in the United States (Oshinsky 2005).

EMERGENCE OF AN INFRASTRUCTURE TO COMBAT POLIO

In 1938 President Roosevelt launched the National Foundation for Infantile Paralysis, which later became commonly known as the March of Dimes, to develop and implement a strategy for alleviating polio and to ensure that people who were already afflicted could receive the best treatment possible. The organization grew rapidly, partially because of its ability to leverage a broad appeal for support to combat a condition that the president, and thousands of others, suffered from.

The organization ultimately became a model of third-sector strategies for addressing medical concerns. Much of its activity was to provide support to researchers whose efforts centered on the third sector. One researcher who received support from the foundation was Dr. Jonas Salk, who was based at the University of Pittsburgh.

Salk's success in identifying a vaccine for polio was based on the concept of a dead virus vaccination. This approach was based on viruses that had been killed but would still trigger an immunity reaction in people who received the vaccination. To test his newly developed vaccine, Salk injected himself, his wife, and his sons. Later examinations suggested that the vaccine had worked on them.

In April 1954, one of the largest vaccination trials in U.S. history was implemented. The Salk polio vaccine was tested in over two hundred counties across the nation. Parents signed consent forms to test the vaccine on their children, and over one million children were given either the dead virus vaccine that Salk and his team had developed or a placebo that would provide a comparison group.

In April of the following year, an announcement at the University of Michigan proclaimed that the Salk vaccination had proved to be effective in a majority of cases, particularly when lined up with results from children who had been injected with a placebo.

Introduction of the vaccine in 1955 had a dramatic effect on epidemic polio in the industrialized world. The victory over polio was for many within the medical establishment an example of the breakthroughs that were emerging with increasing knowledge about infectious disease. It also showed how resources could be mobilized to launch a campaign by drawing largely upon support in the nonprofit sectors to develop a vaccine and then implementing an eradication plan on a wide-scale basis.

The United States witnessed a rapid demonstration of the impact the polio eradication efforts. Between 1956 and 1957, the number of victims dropped from 15,150 to 5,467. By 1961 only 1,312 American children were diagnosed as having infantile paralysis (Kluger 2004, 314). The last case of polio in the United States was in 1979 (ibid., 317).

The March of Dimes' work on polio gave an indication that a network of nongovernmental institutions was gradually becoming positioned to effectively address public health concerns.

The defeat of polio in the United States also permitted researchers to develop strategies for eradicating it in international contexts. In 1988, the World Health Assembly passed a resolution encouraging the World Health Organization member nations to eliminate polio entirely by the year 2000.

While the eradication goal of the year 2000 was ultimately not achieved, significant strides have been made in eliminating the disease. In 1988, there were 350,000 cases of polio worldwide. By 2009, there were an estimated 2,000 cases. In 1988 the nations that were believed to have polio endemic in their populations totaled 125; in 2006 only 4 were noted as having polio endemic: Nigeria, Afghanistan, India, and Pakistan. Finally, it is estimated that the number of children who are walking and not paralyzed, largely because of goals established by the global community, is roughly five million.

SMALLPOX

Smallpox is caused by a virus that spreads through the air and multiplies in the lymph glands. Often an infected victim of smallpox does not show signs of infection until after it has incubated for a week to ten days. The initial symptoms are a high fever and severe aching. After two or three days, a deep rash appears, then develops into small pustules all over the body. Frequently, smallpox would lead to death for the infected person.

History is full of stories telling the impact of smallpox on civilizations around the globe. When Francisco Pizarro arrived in what is now Peru in the 1530s, he found an Inca empire still reeling from an encounter with the disease that ten years earlier had killed almost a third of the population. Smallpox introduced by the Spanish in the 1620s is blamed for reducing native populations in Central America from 25 million to 1.6 million. In the eighteenth century, the disease killed 400,000 people a year in Europe. In the twentieth century, up to half a billion people were killed by the disease. At the same time, by comparison, all the wars on the planet during that time killed roughly 150 million people.

Through the years there have been a number of attempts at combating the impact of smallpox. Then, in 1796, English physician Edward Jenner, in one of the more famous experiments in the history of medicine, inoculated a healthy eight-year-old boy with cowpox—a disease caused by *Vaccinia*, a virus closely related to the *variola* virus—to test the effectiveness of cowpox as a vaccine against smallpox. Jenner's experiment was successful—the boy failed to contract smallpox even when he was deliberately exposed to it.

DEVELOPING AN INFRASTRUCTURE TO COMBAT SMALLPOX

In 1953, Dr. Brock Chisholm, the first director-general of the World Health Organization (WHO), proposed the development of a worldwide program to eradicate smallpox. He argued that WHO had in its hands a large number of statistics, services, and credibility in the global community to expand its efforts beyond the basic areas of surveillance in which it was engaged.

Despite support by some of WHO's individual members, Chisholm's proposal was rejected, as several delegates to the World Health Assembly, the governing body of the WHO, argued that health concerns such as smallpox should be addressed at the national or local levels and not through an international organization's effort.

Five years after Chisholm made his initial proposal, Dr. Viktor Zhdanov, the Soviet Union's deputy health minister, proposed that the WHO director general develop a plan for the eradication of smallpox. The next year, Director-General Marcolino Gomes Candau presented a plan that called for nations where smallpox was endemic to establish a system for 80 percent vaccination. WHO would provide technical assistance when requested. Candau, however, recognizing some of the existing skepticism that smallpox could be eradicated, requested only $100,000 annually for the implementation of such an initiative. In 1959, this modest program was approved, and for several years, minimal resources were dedicated to the smallpox-eradication effort. The results matched those expected from a budget as small as what was provided.

In 1965, President Lyndon Johnson pledged $36.5 million in funding from the United States Agency for International Development (USAID) to help eradicate smallpox from twenty countries in West Africa. That same year, with the support of Johnson's financial commitment, WHO Director-General Candau drew up an extensive plan to present to the World Health Organization for the eradication of smallpox within ten years.

Coupled with the need for funding to enable the plan to work were technological needs. One of the most important technological steps was Dr. Benjamin Rubin's invention of the bifurcated needle in 1965. This instrument consisted of a piece of sharpened steel wire with a double point on one end. It held a very small droplet of the vaccine between its points, and it was efficient, using very little vaccine to get the job done. The needle got a hundred doses of vaccine out of a vial, whereas previously a vial had yielded only twenty-five.

At roughly the same time, new methods were being developed to implement medical procedures. In the early 1950s, Dr. Alexander Langmuir introduced the concept of disease surveillance as a tool in disease prevention. Its application proved to be a vital factor in the smallpox-eradication effort. Langmuir defined surveillance as a program designed to routinely collect relevant data pertaining to a disease, including numbers of cases and deaths;

to analyze and interpret this information; and to distribute it to all responsible for control of the disease in question.

In 1967, the WHO launched its campaign to eradicate smallpox. At the time, two to three million people were dying each year from the disease. The campaign was based on a strategy of circular eradication, whereby when one person was found to be infected, the communities surrounding the person were immunized, with the goal of building a barrier between the infected person and anyone who might be susceptible to the infection.

In 1972, five years after the launch of the campaign, WHO and the Centers for Disease Control in were able to declare that smallpox had been eradicated in the United States. Five years later, in 1977, the last naturally occurring smallpox cases were reported in Somalia.

In 1979, WHO recommended that vaccination against smallpox be stopped in all countries. After intense verification by a commission of prominent scientists in 1979, WHO's global eradication of smallpox was confirmed by the World Health Assembly in 1980.

On May 8, 1980, the World Health Assembly issued a formal declaration that the world had defeated smallpox, emphasizing that this goal had been reached as a result of nations' coordinating with one another to achieve it.

This declaration provided cause for celebration for people in numerous institutions. Smallpox, which had been the cause of death for millions of people over the centuries, was finally eradicated by the institutional capacity to handle the challenges of achieving that goal.

MALARIA

In 1897, Ronald Ross, a British medical officer serving in India, accurately hypothesized that mosquitoes were responsible for transmitting the malaria parasite. His hypothesis, and later work related to it, served as the foundation for a vector-based approach to eradicating malaria.

A few years before Ross drew this conclusion, a member of the U.S. military by the name of William Gorgas was bitten by a mosquito that gave him yellow fever. Unlike many others who contracted this disease, Gorgas survived. Like other survivors, he would consequently be immune to later attacks by yellow fever. His immunity would make him an ideal candidate for assisting with studying outbreaks of yellow fever in various settings. In 1898, Gorgas was assigned by the U.S. government to the position of chief sanitary officer in Cuba, where he would examine factors allowing the transmission of yellow fever.

In Cuba, Gorgas built largely upon the research of Major Walter Reed and Cuban doctor Carlos Findlay, both of whom had developed initial research based on the assumption that mosquitoes were the vectors for the transmission of yellow fever. Under this assumption, Gorgas led a campaign to eradicate mosquitoes in the city of Havana as a strategy for eliminating the presence of yellow fever in the city. With a staff consisting primarily of local Cubans, Gorgas combed the city for any potential breeding grounds for mosquitoes. His staff covered water catchment buckets with wire screens and oiled small pools of water where mosquitoes might have bred.

In 1902, Gorgas wrote to then Surgeon General George Sternberg to share discoveries he and others were making in Havana regarding yellow fever. In the letter, he suggested that much of the work in Havana would probably have an impact upon work taking place in Panama in the building of the Panama Canal. Gorgas pointed out that early attempts by France to build a canal had failed because France had lost one-third of the French laborers working on the canal to yellow fever and malaria (Gorgas 1915, 149). He suggested that if it was possible to protect workers in Panama from yellow fever and malaria, based on what he had learned in Cuba about controlling yellow fever by managing the populations of mosquitoes—recognized as the disease vectors— U.S. efforts to complete the canal would not encounter the losses of the French efforts. After considering Gorgas's letter, Sternberg recommended that Gorgas be placed in charge of mosquito control in Panama.

In March 1904, Gorgas was ordered to accompany the Isthmian Canal Commission, which had been organized under President Theodore Roosevelt to manage the building of the Panama Canal, and to develop plans for protecting workers building the canal from mosquitoes carrying yellow fever and malaria. The challenge was to keep the death toll from malaria and yellow fever to a minimum.

Gorgas and his team launched a multistage approach to control the threat of exposure to the infectious mosquitoes. First his team fumigated every one of the homes of Panama City, a city with a population of 20,000 people at the time. This process entailed the use of 120 tons of insect powder and 300 tons of sulfur (Gorgas 1915, 151). His team then divided the route of the canal into several "sanitary zones," where they cleared brush and undergrowth near homes and villages in the vicinity of the canal and drained potential breeding areas of mosquitoes. Small bodies of water would be oiled, and ditches where mosquitoes might have bred were covered in concrete, thus making them uninhabitable.

This extensive process of controlling the population of mosquitoes ultimately enabled the building to proceed, with a much smaller percentage of fatalities from exposure to malaria and yellow fever than would have occurred had such population control efforts not been undertaken.

The opening of the canal in 1914 was largely the result of being able to manage the challenge of malaria among the workers who were building it. Of the over twenty-six thousand employees working on the canal in 1906, more than twenty-one thousand were hospitalized for malaria or yellow fever at some time during their work. By 1912, due to the incorporation of insect- and malarial-control strategies, as well as the elimination of yellow fever, there were over fifty thousand employees, and the number of hospitalized employees decreased to approximately 5,600 (CDC 2010).

The strategies Gorgas used in Panama would prove useful in the United States in the early 1900s when the advancement of hydroelectric power in many communities increased the amount of water held in dammed river sites. The artificial lakes served as breeding grounds for many of the mosquitoes that would be vectors of malaria.

The 1930s witnessed the development of two methods for managing malaria in the United States. First was the 1934 discovery of chloroquine as an antimalarial drug by scientists at the Bayer laboratories in Germany. While Bayer did not immediately place chloroquine into circulation, it was used heavily by U.S. troops in World War II as they found themselves in areas infested with mosquitoes transmitting malaria. Second was the 1939 identification of the insecticidal elements of dichlorodiphenyltrichloroethane (DDT), which had been discovered in 1874. DDT was a powerful insecticide that was able to eradicate mosquitoes from target areas. Like chloroquine, it was used heavily in World War II to treat areas where troops were active to reduce the cases of malaria among troops.

Coordinating the malaria-control strategies during World War II was the Office of Malarial Control in War Areas, an entity developed to address the challenge of the thousands of military personnel who were being infected by malaria on South Pacific battlefronts. The office also focused on ensuring that those who had been infected by malaria in war zones did not introduce it into their communities when they returned home to the United States.

The end of the war saw the Office of Malarial Control transformed into the Communicable Disease Center, known also as the Center for Disease Control and Prevention (CDC), in 1946. One of this new agency's initial undertakings was a program known as the National Malarial Eradication Program, which it coordinated in collaboration with a number of state health agencies. It focused on encouraging the implementation of home fumigation strategies with DDT as a means of addressing the threat of malaria in the United States. After initiating the effort, the CDC and its partner agencies witnessed a steep decline in the cases of malaria. In 1947, 15,000 cases of malaria were reported. In 1950, after an intensive spraying campaign, only 2,000 cases were reported. By 1951, malaria was presumed to be eliminated from the United States (CDC 2010).

In 1955, with the tools of DDT and chloroquine at its disposal, the World Health Organization launched its own campaign to eradicate malaria from all areas outside of tropical Africa. In 1958, Senators John Kennedy and Hubert Humphrey introduced legislation that allocated $100 million for a five-year worldwide malaria-eradication program. Support for this initiative was sent to the WHO and countries willing to convert their malaria-control programs into malaria-eradication programs. Between 1957 and 1963, the United States spent $490 million on the campaign.

As a result of the WHO-coordinated campaign, 37 of the 143 nations where malaria was endemic in 1950 were free of it by 1978. Other nations where malaria had a strong presence saw dramatic reductions in their cases of malaria. India, which had an estimated 110 million cases of malaria reported in 1955, had fewer than one million in 1968. Sri Lanka witnessed its cases of malaria shrink from an estimated 2.8 million cases reported in 1946 to 18 reported cases in 1966 (Mendis, Rietveld, et al. 2009, 2). Much of the campaign was based on the notion of using heavy amounts of DDT for the control of mosquitoes. In time, another concern grew regarding the safety of DDT use.

The 1962 book *Silent Spring* helped to minimize the use of DDT. In the book, author Rachel Carson argues that DDT was having a negative impact on the lives of people who were absorbing it due to its overuse. *Silent Spring* and several studies on the safety of various pesticides being used in the United States and elsewhere began to raise concerns about their harmful effects. Eventually, despite the initial successes of malaria-eradication programs, these concerns regarding the pesticides caused a reduction in funding for the malaria programs, resulting in a resurgence of malaria in many of the areas targeted for its elimination. By 1969, the goal of malaria eradication was replaced by a broader goal of implementing malaria-control strategies.

Through the 1970s and 1980s, limited financial support and increasing challenges in addressing malaria—DDT-resistant mosquitoes and increasingly chloroquine-resistant malaria—led to reduced support for malarial eradication and control efforts.

REENVISIONING ERADICATION

By the early 1990s, world leaders were recognizing a dramatic upsurge in the number of malaria-related deaths in various parts of the world, particularly in Africa. This awareness led to the adoption of the Global Malaria Control Strategy at a ministerial conference convened by World Health Organization in 1992. Two years later, the United Nations General Assembly endorsed the strategy adopted at the WHO conference.

In 1998, World Health Organization Director-General Gro Brutland proclaimed that "we have enough knowledge, skills, and tools to launch a new concerted effort" against malaria. Brutland's statement coincided with the design and launch of a collaborative effort known as Roll Back Malaria. This campaign aimed to build a collaborative effort among representatives from over five hundred organizations, including governments, multilateral institutions, the nongovernmental sector, and the corporate arena, to secure funding and political commitments around the vision of achieving a malaria-free world.

In Roll Back Malaria's first ten years of operation, three nations—Morocco, Turkmenistan, and the United Arab Emirates—were certified by the WHO as having eliminated malaria within their borders. Additionally, the program has estimated that the lives of over 1.1 million children in Africa have been saved due to its efforts. Finally, WHO estimates that half of the malaria-endemic countries in the regions it has targeted have been able to reduce malaria cases and deaths by 50 percent or more (WHO 2011).

CONCLUSION: OPTIMISM AND CAUTION

At a 1948 gathering of the Fourth International Congress on Tropical Medicine, Secretary of State George C. Marshall declared that the conquest of all infectious disease was imminent (Najera 1989). Three years later, in 1951, the World Health Organization declared that, through careful local management, Asian malaria could soon reach a stage wherein it would be "no longer of major importance" (ibid., 231).

These advances in addressing the challenges of infectious disease were echoed in 1967 by U.S. Surgeon General William H. Stewart, who would tell a White House gathering of state health officers that it was time to shift all national attention and resources from infectious disease to chronic disease, which he and many others viewed as the most important areas for the public health field to emphasize. Stewart's optimism, as well as the optimism of scores of policy makers, that many of the world's infectious diseases had been eradicated led to a shift of focus from research on possible cures for these diseases and to the dismantling of various surveillance processes developed to track and monitor both known and unknown infectious diseases. Over the decades following Stewart's pronouncement, a number of surveillance facilities were closed. The optimism that underscored these pronouncements spoke to the impact of advancements in science, planning processes, and resource mobilization on policy makers' beliefs of what was truly achievable.

Despite these predictions of our final victory over infectious disease, there were some voices of caution. A few researchers were concerned that the optimism was premature. Bacteriologist Rene Dubos, who helped to pioneer the development of antibiotics, warned in 1942:

> It is a dangerous error to believe that disease and suffering can be wiped out altogether by raising still further the standards of living, increasing our mastery of the environment, and developing new therapeutic procedures. The less pleasant reality is that, since the world is ever changing, each period and each type of civilization will continue to have its burden of diseases created by unavoidable failure of biological and social adaptation to counter new threats. (Hunter 2003, 198)

Dubos's concerns were echoed in 1968 by Joseph Lederberg, who had won the Nobel Prize ten years earlier for work on genetic recombination in bacteria and bacterial evolution. Lederberg observed, "The threat of a major virus epidemic—a global pandemic—hangs over the head of the species at any time" (Abraham 2007, 4).

8
HIV/AIDS

"In the past, people used to care for the orphans and loved them," shared the Kenyan grandmother, "but these days they are so many, and many people have died who could have assisted them and therefore orphanhood is a common phenomenon, not strange. The few who are alive cannot support them" (UNICEF 2006, 2). The anonymity of the grandmother, merely an elderly woman quoted in a United Nations Children's Fund (UNICEF) report on HIV/AIDS orphans, suggests that there were many other grandmothers in her community and in communities in other parts of the world who were witnessing firsthand the gravity of HIV/AIDS.

In 2006, the year in which the UNICEF report appeared, projections on the numbers of HIV/AIDS orphans in many nations were cause for immense concern. As a whole, sub-Saharan Africa was predicted to have upward of ten million children who had lost, or within a few years would lose one or both parents due to HIV/AIDS. At country-specific levels, questions of how to support these children as they grew into adults were among the major social concerns of the time.

Since it first emerged on the global landscape in the early 1980s, HIV/AIDS has brought a number of major challenges for communities around the world. A lesson learned, relatively rapidly, was that even though it was initially considered a disease affecting a limited number of population groups, HIV/AIDS is nondiscriminating in who it impacts. Many people around the world of differing cultures, races, and backgrounds have been and will be affected.

This chapter examines the evolution of HIV/AIDS since it appeared as a global public health concern. HIV/AIDS speaks directly to the challenges predicted by public health scholars who warned against the assumption that the days of infectious disease were behind us. Indeed, HIV/AIDS merely demonstrated that we will probably continue to confront new infectious diseases that will require concerted resources from all sectors to combat them.

Since it appeared in the early 1980s, HIV/AIDS has been shown to have a critical impact on society, and there has been an evolution in society's response. New institutions have emerged, new policies have been developed internationally and domestically, and new techniques have developed to shape how communities respond to a medical emergency of this magnitude. To explore the changing nature of the HIV/AIDS crisis, I present decade-by-decade some of the varied societal and institutional responses to it.

HISTORICAL OVERVIEW

"The only thing I really have to give is a good discussion on me," noted Ray Engebretsen, a thirty-seven-year-old lawyer who died of complications related to HIV/AIDS in the mid-1980s. In the last few months of his life, Engebretsen was interviewed in a series of stories for the *Washington Blade*, Washington DC's weekly newspaper serving the city's gay community. The articles on his last few months of living with HIV/AIDS depicted the changes he endured in his physical, social, and economic well-being. He had dropped from one hundred and fifty pounds to ninety pounds. He had lost his job and was living on savings and the assistance of friends. In the July before his death, as he reflected on the realization of his mortality he noted, "Trying to face the reality. It's not in the abstract anymore. It's becoming very real. I asked the doctor. He said maybe days, maybe weeks, a few months. There are many times when I don't want to continue like this for a few months. In this shape I just really don't. But I'm not ready to stop either, so I keep plugging along" ("AIDS: Risks and Responsibilities" 1985).

Engebretsen's reality came within five years of the jubilation that the scientific and medical community was feeling at the announcement of the eradication of smallpox. The timing of HIV/AIDS' surfacing on the global scene engendered a wide-scale discussion on the caution with which the world should regard the optimism that many researchers had been feeling about the elimination of pandemics. As Rene Dubos and Joseph Lederberg had warned, we would confront a number of new challenges in the field of infectious disease.

Less than a year after the declaration by the World Health Organization that smallpox had been eradicated, the June 5, 1981, issue of the CDC's *Morbidity and Mortality Weekly Report* (MMWR), reported news of five homosexual men in their twenties and thirties in Los Angeles who had been diagnosed with *Pneumocystis carinii* (now termed *Pneumocystis jeroveci*), a rare form of pneumonia that tends to affect men who are in their fifties. Over the next several weeks, additional reports would surface of men being affected by either *Pneumocystis carinii* or Kaposi sarcoma, a rare form of skin cancer that also tended to affect men over the age of fifty. Members of the medical research community who read about these cases were puzzled.

Within less than a year, cases of this new disease would increasingly appear around the world, setting off an immediate panic that would impact how we would think about factors of public health. Within a brief period of time, a name for this new disease would be created, acquired immune deficiency syndrome (AIDS), and the agent responsible for it, the human immunodeficiency virus (HIV), would be identified.

1980s: The Appearance and Spread of AIDS

In June 1983, the *New York Times* reported that more than 70 percent of the victims of this new disease were either homosexual or bisexual men. Initially, because of the rates of prevalence in the gay communities, the name given to this condition was gay-related immunodeficiency disease (GRID) (Altman 1982). However, soon other groups were recognized as being infected. Intravenous drug users, people from Haiti, and people who had received blood transfusions were among them.

The first decade of the HIV/AIDS epidemic was shaped by several dynamics that influenced the broader response. First, the public health infrastructure was under major transition. When HIV/AIDS emerged, the Centers for Disease Control was in the middle of an internal debate on the ideal strategy for dealing with public health concerns. A belief in modern medical capabilities led many public officials to argue for decreased spending in areas of public health prevention. This movement was exacerbated by the growing belief that we had halted the spread of infectious disease. Thus, the agency faced the question of how, in the midst of calls for reform and restructuring, it would address a challenge that at the time was viewed as going against a trend of infectious disease elimination.

Second was the impact of the civil rights achievements of the gay rights movement of the early 1970s. Through the early part of the 1970s, the rights and opportunities for members of gay communities across America were expanding. In several cities ordinances were being passed to protect the civil liberties of gay men and women by adding "sexual orientation" to existing antidiscrimination laws. In some instances, standoffs such as those at New York City's Stonewall Inn, where bar patrons stood up to police harassment of gays by launching into several days of protest, led to even more rights. This series of protests helped to raise a political consciousness of gay rights issues and to mobilize people in several cities to focus attention and energy on further advocating for gay rights.

In its early years, gay rights advocates and support groups for people who were HIV positive and/or living with AIDS drew on some of the techniques developed during the 1970s protests to engage advocacy for their mission. In May 1983, the *New York Times* reported that the gay community in New York had already set up an advice center, developed major fund-raising drives, and mobilized its community members to either support or advocate for the needs of people who were HIV-positive.

STIGMAS AND RESPONSES IN THE 1980s

One of the challenges that many of these emergent organizations had to deal with was stigma that was placed on homosexuals by broad segments of society. As Ron Godwin, executive vice president of the right-wing Moral Majority in the early 1980s, declared:

CHAPTER 8

> We feel the deepest sympathy for AIDS victims, but I'm upset that the government is not spending more money to protect the general public from the gay plague. . . . What I see, is a commitment to spend our tax dollars on research to allow these diseased homosexuals to go back to their perverted practices without any standards of accountability. (Shilts 2007, 322)

Godwin's comment spoke to many of the perceptions, spoken and unspoken, that people had about HIV/AIDS and its victims. Increasingly, reports were surfacing of an emergent hysteria around HIV, mixed with demonstrations of thinly masked homophobia. In several instances, landlords evicted tenants who were HIV positive. In New York, hospital staff that had been serving a man who died of AIDS refused to clean his room afterward for fear of contracting the disease. After the man's death, the hospital staff wrapped his body in sheets and placed it in a plastic bag. Undertakers at the funeral home where the body was taken simply poured embalming fluid on top of the sheets, closed the plastic bag, and placed the body in the casket. In San Francisco, the police chief had vinyl gloves and masks issued to over two hundred officers who were afraid of contracting HIV/AIDS (Clendinen 1983).

The hostile reactions and ambivalence in much of the United States regarding the disease and the large number of gay victims led to the development of several advocacy and support mechanisms in the face of the toll on human life and civil liberties. In New York, the Gay Men's Health Crisis enlisted more than one thousand volunteers and raised approximately $1 million in its initial several months of existence. In San Francisco, Chicago, Denver, Houston, and other cities, organizations gathered volunteers to provide counseling, food, housing and financial assistance for AIDS victims. Part of the challenge in the initial years of the spread of HIV was to gain acceptance within the broader medical and political community as an illness that needed attention. In 1987, Randy Shilts, a reporter for the *San Francisco Chronicle*, published an account of the first five years of the AIDS epidemic in a book titled *And the Band Played On*. In the introduction, he notes:

> People died and nobody paid attention because the mass media did not like covering stories about homosexuals and was especially skittish

about stories that involved gay sexuality. Newspapers and television largely avoided discussion of the disease until the death toll was too high to ignore and the casualties were no longer just the outcasts. Without the media to fulfill its role as public guardian, everyone else was left to deal—and not deal—with AIDS as they saw fit. (Shilts 2007, xxiii)

In 1986, a demographic shift occurred in the makeup of people susceptible to HIV/AIDS. In 1986, the Centers for Disease Control reported that a disproportionately high number of cases were from African American and Hispanic populations (CDC 1986). In August of the following year, U.S. Representative Charles Rangel (D-NY) observed, "These groups represent just 18 percent of the overall population, but 39 percent of the AIDS cases. When one considers AIDS cases among children, the figures are much higher, fully 80 percent of children reported with AIDS are non-white" (Rangel 1987).

By the middle of the 1980s, it was also recognized that HIV/AIDS was a challenge facing the whole world. In April 1985, health experts from around the world attended the First International Conference on AIDS in Atlanta, Georgia. This gathering of experts from several major fields affected by AIDS enabled researchers to explore strategies for controlling and preventing the disease.

Immediately following the conference, a World Health Organization committee met to formulate practical responses to the emergent crisis. This meeting was an early and critical step in the development of a global network of institutions focusing on finding a solution to the problem. The World Health Organization's initial strategy was to initiate the Special Program on AIDS, which later became known as the Global Program on AIDS (GPA). In 1988, due to shifting challenges facing both these organizations, GPA merged with the United Nations Development Program (UNDP), in anticipation that the merger would lead to enhanced coordinated strategies, drawing upon several resources.

1990s: The Second Decade of HIV/AIDS

By the early 1990s, HIV/AIDS was recognized as a disease that was touching many communities throughout the United States and was not discriminating in picking its target. In July 1990, the *Journal of the American Medical Association* noted that AIDS is "rapidly rising nationally as a cause of death among women aged 15 to 44 years old, and is the leading killer of black women in that age group in New York and New Jersey." Eight years later, the *New York Times* reported that while African Americans made up 13 percent of the U.S. population, they accounted for 57 percent of all new infections of HIV/AIDS. With such statistics, it was becoming safe to say that HIV/AIDS was heavily affecting the nation's African American population. In response to these statistics, Surgeon General David Satcher noted, "I don't think there is any question that the epidemic in this country is becoming increasingly an epidemic of color" (Stolberg 1998).

One of the crucial questions at the time was why the infection rate in minority communities was as large as it was. Socioeconomics played a part in the answer, particularly when examining some of the correlations between poverty and the HIV/AIDS rates. In addition, these questions fell at the same time the crack epidemic of the late 1980s and 1990s was making its way across various cities—also having a disproportionate impact on African American communities. Crack's impact in many areas was to increase rates of prostitution, due largely to the desperation of many who were addicted to it and a willingness to go to great lengths to obtain money for the drug.

An additional reason that the occurrence was becoming disproportionate in African American communities was an unwillingness of many of the institutions, primarily the churches and civic groups within African American communities, to acknowledge and work on the issue of HIV/AIDS as a pressing problem.

In contrast, one of the immediate reactions in many of the nation's gay communities was to develop an infrastructure of organizations at the national and local levels to advocate for and support members of many of these communities who were HIV positive.

Internationally, on January 1, 1996, the Joint United Nations Program on HIV/AIDS (UNAIDS) was launched in an attempt to draw upon the experience and skills of all United Nations agencies to battle the disease. The organization was originally composed of six cosponsoring agencies, including the United Nations Children's Fund (UNICEF), the United Nations Development Program (UNDP), the United Nations Population Fund (UNFPA), the United Nations Educational, Scientific and Cultural Organization (UNESCO), the World Health Organization (WHO), and the World Bank. Also the office of secretariat was established, to be responsible for administering the organization and providing centralized management functions. It was a global infrastructure that would help shape a collaborative response to this challenge.

Twenty-First Century

The initial decade of the twenty-first century witnessed continued concerns about HIV/AIDS in minority communities in the United States. Much of the emphasis was particularly on the impact of HIV/AIDS on African American women and Hispanics. According to a report by the Centers for Disease Control, in 2003, the rate of new AIDS cases for black women was twenty times that of white women and five times greater than the infection rate for Latinas. In 2003, the National Black Leadership Commission on AIDS reported, based partially on the CDC's data, that African American and Hispanic women represented 83 percent of all reported AIDS diagnoses among women, although they represented only 25 percent of all women. According to the report, AIDS was among the three top causes of death for black women ages thirty-five to forty-four.

At the beginning of the new millennium, HIV/AIDS continued to be seen as a global issue that would need to leverage additional resources from around the world. In April 2000, UN Secretary-General Kofi Annan called for a tenfold increase in funding for AIDS relief from developed nations. Annan suggested that a "war chest" of $7–10 billion be spent annually, almost ten times what had previously been spent in any year of the last two decades. Although specifically citing concern over the proliferation of AIDS across Africa, in an effort to make the increase more politically feasible Annan announced that the increase would be targeted not only at AIDS alone, but also toward tuberculosis and malaria, infectious diseases that also were responsible for the deaths of millions of people annually. The new fund was envisioned as a mechanism to provide better coordination of efforts to confront AIDS, promote transparency to the distribution of resources, and decentralize decision making in regard to program design and implementation.

In May 2001, the Global Fund to Fight HIV/AIDS, Tuberculosis, and Malaria was established in Belgium as an independent legal entity registered under Swiss law. The Global Fund was established not as a traditional intergovernmental organization but more as a nongovernmental organization that had a commitment of support from a number of donor nations that would be involved with financing its development over the years. The Global Fund would ultimately become one of the central institutions globally that would address the crisis of HIV/AIDS.

A year and a half after the Global Fund was established, in September 2002, the U.S. National Intelligence Council released a report titled "The Next Wave of HIV/AIDS." The report suggested that the spread of HIV/AIDS would be of considerable concern in Nigeria, Ethiopia, Russia, India, and China. The NIC singled out those countries for several reasons: They were among some of the world's most populous states, comprising some 40 percent of the world's population; they were all of strategic importance to the United States; they were in the early to middle stages of the epidemic; and they were all led by governments that have not yet given the issue the sustained high priority that has been key to stemming the tide of the disease in other countries. The report projected numbers for the next-wave countries to the decade's end: infections in the five countries would grow from current levels of around 14–23 million to an estimated 50–75 million by 2010. Combining the next-wave countries and central and southern Africa, even excluding the rest of the world, brought the 2010 NIC estimate to 80–110 million infections. The clarity of the report for policy makers provided a basis to justify additional governmental, nongovernmental, and intergovernmental actions to address what had become a major health crisis of the late twentieth and early twenty-first centuries.

CONCLUSION

The end of the twenty-first century's first decade saw some positive news related to the spread of HIV/AIDS. According to the

2010 UNAIDS report, between 1999 and 2010 the number of new infections had fallen by 19 percent. The report also noted that of the estimated 15 million people living with HIV in low- and middle-income countries who needed treatment, 5.2 million had access to it—translating into fewer AIDS-related deaths.

Several months after the release of the UNAIDS report, the world marked the thirtieth anniversary of the CDC's 1981 Morbidity and Mortality Weekly Report that first made much of the world aware of HIV/AIDS. In the years since, HIV/AIDS has dramatically affected the world. Health systems have responded by developing new policies and procedures to address the issue. Societies also have had to wrestle with the vast realities of what they should do when large segments of their populations are no longer around due to HIV/AIDS.

One of the pressing lessons from HIV/AIDS is its demonstration of what can happen when a new infectious disease is not quickly addressed. With HIV/AIDS, we witnessed the rapid spread of an infection, and for a number of years there was limited government and intergovernmental action in response. As a result, in the early twenty-first century we face a world without the countless people who have been lost due to the inability to develop effective responses to HIV/AIDS. We also find ourselves wrestling with questions of whether we would identify strategies for responding to new infectious diseases as we became aware of them or if we would make a similar mistake of responding slowly if again confronted with an outbreak of a major infection.

9

Anticipated Health Crises

On April 1, 2003, twenty buses pulled to the front of Block E of Amoy Gardens, a residential complex consisting of ten thirty-five-story-tall buildings in Hong Kong. Residents were loaded onto the buses and driven to an isolated facility where over the next few weeks they were kept in quarantine and monitored for changes in the status of their health. In the days preceding the evacuation, Amoy Gardens Block E had been recognized as a central location in which people infected with severe acute respiratory syndrome (SARS) lived. In time, it was discovered that over one-third of the SARS cases in Hong Kong came from this particular housing complex.

In the early part of 2003, doctors, scientists, and policy makers around the world found themselves wrestling with SARS, an infectious disease that the World Health Organization later recognized as the first "severe infectious disease to emerge in the 21st century" (WHO 2003). Within a matter of eight months, SARS infected over eight thousand people in over thirty countries. More than seven hundred of the infections proved fatal.

SARS arrived at a moment when the international health community was recognizing that it needed to adjust its strategies for confronting infectious disease. Its arrival slightly over two decades after the global emergence of HIV/AIDS left health institutions confronting a new infectious disease and the question of how the global health community could respond to new public-health threats. Five major concerns marked the emerging policy discourse around SARS.

First, the SARS crisis became a factor in the World Health Organization's refinement of its role in addressing global health concerns. As a global organization founded in the late 1940s that had evolved slowly, the World Health Organization faced a number of challenges in addressing the outbreak of SARS, particularly issues of enforcement in a major health crisis. How successfully could WHO impose a set of procedures upon sovereign nations facing the dangers of SARS? Another test was whether WHO had adequate surveillance capabilities. Did the organization have ample means for identifying and tracking the movement of SARS across national boundaries? As WHO explored these critical issues, it needed to do so while dealing with the dynamics of a very real and present public health issue.

Second, SARS gave rise to concerns about governments' response to a public health threat. At the beginning of the SARS outbreak, China, the nation where SARS originated, minimized the flow of information to the public about the disease. Ultimately, it was not until several months after the initial outbreak that China issued information about it. Had such information been shared earlier, much of it could probably have been used to minimize the spread of the infection in China and other nations. In time, the government's lack of transparency on the SARS outbreak was viewed as one of the reasons that the virus was not contained in its early stages. China's conduct raised questions of a government's obligations to report a public health concern.

Third, SARS has come to represent challenges related to animal-to-human viral leaps. Infectious diseases are increasingly being viewed as stemming from viruses that leap between species. In the case of HIV/AIDS, the commonalities between simian immunodeficiency virus (SIV) and human immunodeficiency virus (HIV) suggest that the origin of HIV/AIDS may have been in primates. In the case of the flu viruses of 1918, 1957, 1968, and 2004 epidemics, birds are widely believed to be the sources of these viruses. In the case of SARS, it was originally believed to have been from civet cats sold in live animal markets in China, where the virus originated. A subsequent theory is that bats were the carriers.

Fourth, SARS represents how a new diseases can spread in an era of enhanced transportation. As we learned with SARS, it is quite easy for a disease to quickly spread to several locations via our modern-day facility to move from place to place globally in short amounts of time. In a brief period, cases of SARS arose in several countries.

Finally, SARS provided the challenge of minimizing the spread of disease in the face of late-modern urban population growth. As more people come to live in urban rather than rural settings, governments will need to figure out how to deter the spread of infectious disease in areas with a high population density. Several of the cities where SARS appeared had to implement quarantine measures to prevent it from infesting the urban setting.

The questions raised by SARS cut across a number of areas of concern relating to public safety, the protection of civil liberties, and the development of infrastructures and how to effectively respond to a major health crisis and prepare for future emerging infectious diseases. They also added to the discussion of how challenges of emergent infectious disease might be addressed in the twenty-first century.

GLOBAL HEALTH SURVEILLANCE

In 1951, the World Health Organization adopted its International Sanitary Regulations. Renamed the International Health Regulations (IHR) in 1956, these regulations were established to help prevent the international spread of disease. Countries have numerous obligations under the regulations, including a duty to report outbreaks of certain communicable diseases in their territories.

In 1969, the IHR were adapted to prevent the spread of diseases internationally through an early detection system. The current regulations are intended to help monitor and control six infectious diseases: cholera, plague, yellow fever, smallpox, relapsing fever, and typhus. The regulations provide that investigation of disease outbreaks within countries is the responsibility of each individual country. However, for three specific diseases with implications for international health—plague, cholera, and yellow fever—countries are to report cases to WHO as quickly as possible.

In the early 1990s, much of the global public health community became increasingly concerned about the emergence of new infectious diseases. Part of this concern stemmed from experiences with HIV/AIDS, Ebola, and many of the other new diseases that were beginning to appear at the end of the twentieth century. These new diseases, as well as an enhanced understanding of viral mutation and adaptation, raised a number of questions on the next type of virus that would develop.

In May 1995, driven partially by a growing consensus that new infectious diseases were coming to light, the World Health Assembly, the policy and decision-making body of the WHO, passed one of its first resolutions on emerging infections. It called upon the World Health Organization to develop plans to improve the global capacity for identifying emerging infections. It also called for its member states to enhance their health surveillance infrastructures.

A direct outgrowth of this call for action was the development of the WHO's Global Health Intelligence Network (GPHIN) in 1996 to scan the Internet for rumors and reports of suspicious disease events. Four years following the development of the GPHIN, the World Health Organization developed the Global Outbreak Alert and Response Network (GOARN). GOARN consists of specialized personnel who can be rapidly deployed for epidemiological investigations and assistance in the event of some form of public health outbreak.

With the development of these two networks, the World Health Organization had the means for monitoring and responding to outbreaks of infectious disease in ways that were more effective than it had yielded before—an indication that the global health community realized the need to build a means of early detection, warning, and rapid coordination in the response to emergent infectious diseases.

EMERGENCE, SPREAD, AND CYCLE OF SARS

In late 2002, a forty-six-year-old government official in China's Guangdong Province developed a high fever and a cough, which later turned into a severe case of pneumonia. Before being admitted to a hospital for his then unidentifiable illness, he infected five members of his family with the ailment. Several weeks later, another man, this time roughly one hundred miles north of the first, was admitted to a hospital with the same symptoms. This patient left a trail of infected people in the hospital. Within a few more weeks, another individual began a spread of the sickness by another infected individual into three more hospitals. Ultimately, over twenty doctors and nurses who had treated or come into contact with him fell ill.

Guangdong Province, where this series of infections initially spread, is located in southeast China. It is considered one of the critical centers for China's present industrial revolution and is home to nearly 10 million migrant workers, many of whom have moved to the area from China's less industrialized rural areas. The province has also been the point of origin for a number of influenzas and other infectious diseases over the years. In 1957, a new influenza strain emerged from the region and led to that year's flu pandemic. Eleven years later a strain of flu in 1968 emerged from the region and spread to other parts of the world.

In China at the time of these late-2002 outbreaks, disease surveillance was regulated by the National Law on Communicable Disease Prevention and Control, which had previously been revised in 1989. This law mandated reporting of specified diseases and required that each level of government receive reports of these diseases and investigate them. Reports were submitted to higher levels at fixed periods (immediate for Category A diseases, as soon as possible for category B diseases, at the end of the year for Category C diseases). Under the law, if one level was not able to investigate and resolve a disease report, it would request support from the next higher level. Normally, counties, prefectures, and provinces tried to handle disease outbreaks themselves, calling in help only if there were insufficient technical resources to control the disease.

SARS, which did not fall under the listed notifiable diseases, was investigated by local health officials in Guangdong. With no specific legal requirement in the initial stages to report to the central level, government health officials minimized their reports of the severity of the outbreak. Local officials opted to censor the release of information on this outbreak instead of broadcasting information to the public. The only reports that could be published were those from government departments. The local government also decided to keep schools and factories open throughout the crisis.

On February 11, 2003, after an anonymous text message had been broadcast the day before in China about the respiratory illness, the Guangdong provincial government held a press conference acknowledging the presence of the disease and providing some figures on the numbers of cases. According to these official estimates, as of February 5, there had been 305 cases of this mysterious illness, resulting in five deaths. Among the individuals affected were 105 health-care workers. Two months later, in late February, 688 cases were reported in the province, followed by 364 cases in March and 259 cases in April (Abraham 2007, 25).

HONG KONG

In mid-February 2003, a doctor from Guangdong checked into a room in Hong Kong's Metropole Hotel. Unknown to him, while interacting with a patient in his hometown, he had picked up the SARS virus. While at the Metropole, he fell ill and inadvertently infected at least twelve other people staying in the hotel. Those twelve people in turn helped to spread the illness to others in Hong Kong, Vietnam, Singapore, Ireland, Germany, and Canada. A young Hong Kong resident who visited a friend at the Metropole Hotel on the day the SARS-infected doctor was in residence was later admitted to Hong Kong's Prince of Wales Hospital, where he started an outbreak among doctors, nurses, students, patients, visitors, and relatives. Eventually, this outbreak in the hospital resulted in one hundred cases.

In March 2003, Hong Kong officials announced that a large cluster of cases had occurred almost simultaneously in the Amoy Gardens complex. Up to this point, transmission appeared to have occurred primarily through the respiratory route, but the Amoy Gardens outbreak now raised the possibility that environmental transmissions might also play a key role. An investigation conducted by the Hong Kong authorities identified a faulty sewage system as the probable means of spreading the virus in the building complex. The initial case was identified as a man being treated for kidney disease at a large Hong Kong hospital; he had developed symptoms of SARS while he was visiting his brother at the apartment complex. The evacuation of the towers was one of the first instances, in recent years, of a major evacuation due to the spread of an infectious disease.

In mid-March, WHO officials were informed of the death of a forty-three-year-old man in Toronto, who had just flown back from Hong Kong, where he had stayed in the Metropole Hotel. The man had reported symptoms similar to those of other SARS victims. He ultimately died in a hospital in Canada. His mother and wife had died of the same illness one week earlier. Six of the first ten cases that surfaced in Canada were from this family. Their family doctor became the seventh victim, and although she recovered, an elderly man who happened to be in the hospital emergency department at the same time as one of the family members caught the virus and died. The microbe then moved out into the greater Toronto area, infecting 438 and killing 43 before its spread was finally halted.

One of the pressing questions faced by the international health community was whether or not to implement travel advisories for nations where SARS had been identified. Beginning in March 2003, the World Health Organization began issuing advisories for Hong Kong, Vietnam, Singapore, and China. In time an advisory would be issued for travelers going to Toronto. This was the first time since its founding that the World Health Organization issued travel advisories.

Over time, strategies to address SARS were undertaken at local levels and consisted largely of case-isolation procedures and close monitoring of people that the infected person may have had contact with during periods of disease incubation or infection.

In late May, Singapore became the first of the nations where SARS had appeared to be taken off WHO's list of infected areas. Over the next several months, other nations that had encountered outbreaks of infection were removed as well.

THE SCIENCE OF SARS

By late March, the coordinated efforts of the scientific community began to yield results when scientists at the CDC and in Hong Kong announced that a new coronavirus has been isolated from patients with SARS (CDC 2003). The ability to identify this virus was partly due to a global health network that enabled research-ers from a number of settings to share information though digital communications means that were unlike others used previously. Once the virus was identified, scientists were also able to search for the source of the virus from wherever they were. Advances in global communications enabled a worldwide network of re-searchers to engage in identifying and isolating cases and framing immediate protocols for handling them.

The network of researchers also helped to identify what ul-timately was believed to be the animal host of the SARS virus. Scientists initially traced the SARS virus to the civet cat, an animal found in live animal markets such as those in Guangdong. The initial tracing of SARS to the civet cat raises a number of criti-cal questions regarding animal-to-human leaps, in light of the degree of interaction between animals and humans in domestic, agricultural, and laboratory settings. Increasingly, scientists are recognizing that viruses that evolve in an animal setting may leap between species, causing an adverse and deadly impact in the new host species.

CONCLUSIONS: MODERN ERA FEARS

In the eight months between the first cases that were reported to the declaration that SARS had been contained, more than eight thousand people were infected in over thirty-two countries. More than seven hundred of the cases had proven fatal. As one of the first truly global health scares of the twenty-first century, SARS provides another framework for handling questions regarding public health crises. It appeared as the result of a viral mutation, which is a risk we continuously face—particularly in areas where we interact with other species. It also demonstrated the challenges of viral dissemination in an era of easy, speedy transport and mass urbanization—both of which are increasingly characteristic of the twenty-first century.

There are also a number of questions regarding the duty of governmental transparency. In addressing the outbreak of SARS, China did not respond to the crisis in a way that informed members of both the public and the international community as the disease was initially emerging. One question is how much transparency on the part of the government about the SARS infections would have ultimately been useful in identifying means for addressing the problem.

SARS also provided an opportunity to test the effectiveness of surveillance and response systems established to curb outbreaks of infectious disease in the twenty-first century. The Global Health Intelligence Network helped to identify a new infectious disease concern. The Global Outbreak Alert and Response Network helped to provide an international team of experts who rapidly responded to the issue in ways far more coordinated than in earlier responses to health threats. The speed with which information was shared, after the initial hesitation of the provincial government in Guangdong, and the speedy mobilization of resources ensured that SARS did not spread to a much wider population than it did.

Part III

Technology, Science, and Crisis

On March 28, 2008, scientists Luis Sancho and Walter Wagner filed a request for a permanent injunction against several federal and international agencies supporting the work of the European Center for Nuclear Research (CERN) on the CERN Large Hadron Collider, the world's largest particle accelerator. With the collaborative support of over ten thousand scientists and engineers from around the globe, the device was one of the most complex scientific experiments the world has ever known. Through forcing the collision of subatomic particles, the Hadron Collider aimed to help answer some of the core questions in the worlds of theoretical and applied physics as related to the founding of the universe.

Sancho and Wagner, along with other scientists opposing the Hadron Collider, noted several concerns with the its development. Competing theories predicted doomsday scenarios of what might occur when atoms collided under the planned research effort. Two scenarios were particularly worrisome. The first predicted the creation of new forms of matter known as "strangelets." Such new atomic creations would hypothetically be able to fuse with other forms of matter. Converting matter would join into even larger strangelets. Ultimately, continued and repeated links "would result in a runaway fusion reaction, eventually converting all of Earth into a single 'strangelet' of immense size" (*Luis Sancho v. U.S. Department of Energy* 2008, 4). A second scenario predicted that the collision of two atoms at nearly light speed would create an implosion that would result in the creation of a miniature black hole. In time, such a black hole would absorb all matter coming into contact with it, including ultimately Earth itself.

On September 10, 2008, with the attempted injunction denied, CERN scientists launched the collider. The initial test that day proved successful in avoiding the doomsday scenarios predicted. Nine days later, however, a small explosion in the instrument controlling the collider vaporized one of the electrical connections, and tons of helium were displaced under the Swiss-French countryside. Despite this clear demonstration that error was possible, by August of the following year, reports were published of plans under way to have the Hadron Collider operating again within several months. It was up and running on November 20, 2009.

The Hadron Collider may be perceived as a manifestation of technological determinism—a belief that if technology enables us to pursue certain goals, these goals should be pursued. The optimism that comes with technologically determinate frameworks is coupled with an presumably unpopular possibility: each advancement brings a potential harm to the broader society. With the increasing complexity of technology come potential dangers. Such dangers in the long run may be limitless in their geographical stretch and in their potential harm to humankind and the world in which we live.

A critical balance exists between the benefits of technological advancement and our conceptualizations of risk. The chapters in this section examine this balance. I begin with an examination of risk in a nuclear-armed world. The scientific developments of the twentieth century that enabled us to tap into the potential of nuclear energy promised numerous opportunities for our understanding of the world of physics. One of the challenges that surfaced was the lethal capabilities in the use of such power for belligerent purposes. On two occasions, we have witnessed the use of these capabilities in war. We have also had to contend with the need to ensure that such capabilities would not be used for military purposes again.

I continue with an examination of the challenges of civilian nuclear energy production. This area of scientific technology augured great potential for many individuals at the beginning of the nuclear era as they considered some of the foreseen and unforeseen challenges of nuclear energy. The use of nuclear power has enabled us to tap into seemingly limitless sources of energy and provide power for millions of homes and businesses. However, we also learned that such capabilities bring with them tremendous possibilities for failure. Several serious accidents, including Three

Mile Island in 1979, Chernobyl in 1986, and Fukushima in 2011, provide examples of diasters that can result from risk.

The next chapter explores the risks and liabilities involving toxic waste. Here, I focus on the Love Canal disaster of the late 1970s and the impact it had on the development of policies pertaining to hazardous waste management. I explore questions about the dumping of toxic materials and the liabilities related to such activity.

The issue of risks and liabilities resulting from industrial activity continues in the next chapter, where I examine the 1986 gas leak at the Bhopal plant in India. The leak, which is now recognized as one of the worst industrial accidents ever, immediately killed more than two thousand people in India and caused many thousands of additional deaths and injuries over time. The case of Bhopal raises a number of important questions regarding industrial liabilities when actors are working across national settings, which in an era of increasing international joint ventures is of growing concern.

I close the section with an examination of risk and oil exploration. In contemplating the growing level of oil consumption in the world, we have had to confront the risks of oil exploration and transport, particularly as we have identified oil in increasingly remote locations. I draw upon three cases: the Long Beach oil spill of 1969, the *Exxon Valdez* spill in Alaska's Prince William Sound in 1989, and the Deepwater Horizon spill in the Gulf of Mexico in 2010. Each of these incidents has given us reason to pause and ask questions about the costs both in terms of our own safety and of the broader environment due to our levels of oil consumption.

Ultimately, the cases in this section seek to explore the overriding questions of various late-modern advances as well as provide a broad comprehension of the spread of risks during this era of rapid technological and industrial advancement. They speak largely to questions of crisis specifically in a late-modern era— an era when technological advancement has become a central component of the risk factors that underlie disasters.

10

The Multiple Crises of a Nuclear Era

"The history of mankind is the history of the attainment of external power," noted H.G. Wells in the prelude to his 1914 book, *The World Set Free* (Wells 1914, 11). As he did in many of his other writings, Wells was able to forecast some of the scientific advances of the next several decades and weigh some of the challenges that might come with the expansion of scientific knowledge taking place in his time. Wells's focus in *The World Set Free* was on the ability to build upon the advancement of theories in physics and predict some of the challenges of the nuclear era, an era that was driven by a desire not only for the attainment of external power, but also for its use in both a militaristic and civilian context.

Nearly twenty years after the publication of *The World Set Free*, one of the book's admirers, physicist Leo Szilard, was able to conceive of a process for developing a chain of nuclear reactions. Building upon the work of such pioneers in the world of theoretical physics and chemical sciences as John Dalton, A.R. Newlands, and Pierre and Marie Curie, Szilard and many of his colleagues would help launch the world into the nuclear age. The opportunities and risks of this age would mirror some of the scenarios that Wells described. The development of this age and the risks of the military use of nuclear capabilities serve as the focus of this chapter.

The contributions of several of the scientists who helped to usher in this nuclear era serve as this chapter's starting point. I begin with an examination of their work in the context of the lead-up to the race to develop nuclear weaponry in the early 1940s. Their work ultimately led to the nuclear bombs in Hiroshima and Nagasaki.

The research of these scientists also helped put into motion many of the dangers of an escalated nuclear race, which shaped much of the latter half of the twentieth century—a time when the United States and the then Soviet Union maintained nuclear arsenals that had the capability to destroy the world many times over. Balanced with the political questions that underscored the cold war era were many warnings of the serious risk of humankind's self-annihilation in a nuclear world. These levels of discourse are the basis for exploring the possibilities in a post–cold war era of discovering strategies for minimizing the threats of nuclear weaponry, focusing on the risks of wide-scale weapons proliferation.

History and Scientific Advancement in a Nuclear Era

It is probably a good thing that the residents of Chicago didn't know what was happening in the squash court under the University of Chicago's Stagg Field in the early 1940s. That was where Enrico Fermi, a physicist who had won the 1938 Nobel Prize for his work demonstrating both the existence of new radioactive elements and various forms of nuclear reactions, was focusing on how to control fusion for the secret Manhattan Project. The task of his team was to build, and ultimately test, what was to become the world's first nuclear reactor.

Prior to Fermi's experiments under Stagg Field, physicists around the world debated on both the possibilities and the processes involving controlled fission. In the midst of these debates, Fermi's calculations proved correct—much to Chicago's good fortune—and in turn helped to develop some of the critical phases of the nuclear era.

The approval of government resources for Fermi's experiment was the result of news that had reached Leo Szilard several years earlier that physicists Otto Hahn and Fritz Straussman had succeeded in splitting the atom in Germany in the late 1930s. Upon learning of this achievement, Szilard immediately foresaw the danger of Nazi Germany's developing a weapon based on Hahn and Straussman's atomic work before the rest of the world did. Sensing that Hitler's intentions were to use such capabilities to increase his expansion in Europe, Szilard convinced his mentor,

121

Albert Einstein, to codraft a letter in August of 1939 to be sent under Einstein's signature to President Roosevelt. The letter ultimately
became one of the critical pieces of correspondence in the history
of the nuclear age and pointed to the possibility of a nuclear chain
reaction. As Szilard and Einstein warned Roosevelt:

> This new phenomenon would also lead to the construction of bombs,
> and it is conceivable—though much less certain—that extremely
> powerful bombs of a new type may thus be constructed. A single
> bomb of this type, carried by boat and exploded in a port, might very
> well destroy the whole port together with some of the surrounding
> territory. (Kelly 2007, 43)

It was largely the influence of this letter and the question of
Hitler's nuclear intentions that led Roosevelt to perceive the importance of launching what would ultimately become a race for
the militarization of nuclear capabilities. In October of the same
year, Roosevelt assigned an advisory board, consisting of the
head of the Bureau of Standards and representatives from the
Army and Navy, to explore the possibilities presented by this
new technology. Two months later, Roosevelt further confirmed
the importance of Sziland's warning by ordering the formation
of a Uranium Advisory Committee on December 6, 1941, the day
before the Japanese attack on Pearl Harbor, to determine the cost
and feasibility of creating a bomb.

DEVELOPMENT

At the time of Roosevelt's exchange with Einstein and Szilard,
one of the greatest thinkers in the world of theoretical physics
was J. Robert Oppenheimer. Serving as a faculty member at the
University of California at Berkeley and the California Institute of
Technology, Oppenheimer had been doing research on fast neu-
trons, calculating how much material might be needed for a bomb
and how efficient it might be. In May 1942, Arthur H. Compton,
one of President Roosevelt's key science advisers and head of
the National Academy of Sciences Committee to Evaluate Use of
Atomic Energy in War, chose Oppenheimer to head the scientific
group exploring the feasibility of building an atomic bomb.

In 1942 the efforts that Compton had been overseeing were turned over to the army to manage and renamed the Manhattan Engineering District or the Manhattan Project. Running this effort was Major General Leslie Groves, a West Point graduate who had been involved with a number of projects for the Army Corps of Engineers.

FROM COMMITTEE TO MANHATTAN PROJECT

For the next several years, under tremendous secrecy, Groves and Oppenheimer assembled some of the nation's best minds in science and engineering to work on this new project of weaponizing atomic energy. Today, the effort that resulted is noted as one of the major mobilizations of scientific resources experienced by the United States.

It was the work of the Manhattan Project scientists that laid the foundation for the application of nuclear power in a military and a civilian context. Completion of the Manhattan Project required the coordination of efforts at secret locations in eastern Tennessee, northern New Mexico, and eastern Washington State. In addition, research was conducted at a handful of university research labs, including the lab under Stagg Field where Fermi built his nuclear reactor. The project also involved managing a scientific project across a population of researchers who were not entirely aware of the project being developed. The majority of the people working on the project didn't know what they were working on until after the first atomic bomb was dropped on August 6, 1945.

MOVEMENT TOWARD USE OF THE BOMB

By late 1944, several of the scientists who were aware of the scope and intended use of the project began to voice concerns about it. In the summer of 1945, over 150 scientists signed a petition, drafted by Leo Szilard, to Secretary of War Henry Stimson and President Harry Truman recommending against the bomb's unannounced use against Japan:

> The development of atomic power will provide the nations with new means of destruction. The atomic bombs at our disposal represent

only the first step in this direction, and there is almost no limit to the destructive power which will become available in the course of their future development. Thus a nation which sets the precedent of using these newly liberated forces of nature for purposes of destruction may have to bear the responsibility of opening the door to an era of devastation on an unimaginable scale. . . . If after the war a situation is allowed to develop in the world which permits rival powers to be in uncontrolled possession of these new means of destruction, the cities of the United States as well as the cities of other nations will be in continuous danger of sudden annihilation. All the resources of the United States, moral and material, may have to be mobilized to prevent the advent of such a world situation. Its prevention is at present the solemn responsibility of the United States—singled out by virtue of her lead in the field of atomic power. (Kelly 2007, 292)

On July 26, 1945, the United States, China, and Great Britain issued the Potsdam Proclamation, which gave Japan an ultimatum: immediate unconditional surrender or face "complete and utter destruction." The Japanese rejection of the ultimatum three days later set the final stage for dropping the atomic bombs. On the morning of August 6, the first atomic bomb, Little Boy, was dropped from the *Enola Gay* over Hiroshima.

MILITARY USE

"My God, what have we done," wrote *Enola Gay* copilot Robert A. Lewis, shortly after the release of the first atomic bomb. Crew member Bob Carson gave an account of what occurred forty-three seconds after the bomb was dropped:

> A column of smoke rising fast. It has a fiery red core. A bubbling mass, purple-gray in color, with that red core. It's all turbulent. Fires are springing up everywhere, like flames shooting out of a huge bed of coals. I am starting to count the fires. One, two, three, four, five, six . . . fourteen, fifteen . . . it's impossible. There are too many to count. Here it comes, the mushroom shape that Captain Parsons spoke about. . . . It's like a mass of bubbling molasses. The mushroom is spreading out. It's maybe a mile or two wide and half a mile high. It's nearly level with us and climbing. It's very black, but there is a purplish tint in the cloud. The base of the mushroom looks like a heavy undercast that is shot through with flames. The city must be below that. The flames

and smoke are billowing out, whirling out into the foothills. All I can see now of the city is the main dock and what looks like an airfield. (Clarfield and Wiecek 1984, 54)

Within moments, Hiroshima was transformed into a scorched wasteland that would embed the possibilities of nuclear devastation in the consciousness of the world. More than 130,000 people were killed immediately. Another 70,000 would die from injuries or radiation poisoning by 1950, bringing the total fatalities of Hiroshima to over 200,000 people.

On August 9, 1945, three days after the bombing of Hiroshima, a second atomic bomb was dropped on Nagasaki, killing an additional 73,000 people at once. Like Hiroshima, Nagasaki would result in both short- and long-term harm to people in the vicinity where the bomb struck.

Stories from the ground of both Hiroshima and Nagasaki provide testimony to the damage caused by these weapons. As one person in Hiroshima at the time of the blast remembered:

When the blow came, I closed my eyes but I could still feel the extreme heat. It was like being roasted alive many times over. I noticed that the side of my body was very hot. It was on fire. I tried to put it out, but it would not go out so easily. You could hardly recognize me, my lips and my face were all popped up and I had to force my eyes open with my fingers in order to see. (Allison 2005, 50)

And as told by another blast survivor:

I looked at the face to see if I knew her. It was a woman of about forty. A gold tooth gleamed in the wide open mouth. A handful of singed hair hung down from the left temple over her cheek, dangling in her mouth. Her eyelids were drawn up, showing black holes where the eyes had been burned out. (Allison 2005, 51)

The bombing of Hiroshima and Nagasaki would provide the world with evidence of the destruction possible with nuclear weaponry and would ultimately serve as a deterrent for its use in the minds of many citizens. The bombing of the two cities proved to the world that humankind had within its power the technological capability and willingness to create and use weapons of tremendous force; visual imagery and first-hand accounts confirmed the horrendous destruction. We had witnessed the potential of the nuclear era. How we would manage such capabilities would come to light in our decision making in the postwar era.

THE COLD WAR ERA AND NUCLEAR RISK

The world after Hiroshima and Nagasaki was one in which the major global powers faced critical decisions about how they would choose to interact with one another. Central to the postwar world were relations between the United States and the Soviet Union, nations with a tremendous mistrust of one another.

In 1947, *Foreign Affairs* published one of the wider known articulations of U.S. policy toward the Soviet Union in an article entitled "The Sources of Soviet Conduct," written by foreign policy analyst George Kennan (then writing under the pseudonym X). The article suggested that the "main element of any United States policy toward the Soviet Union must be that of a long-term, patient but firm and vigilant containment of Russian expansive tendencies" (X 1947, 575). This approach coincided with the launch of the Truman Doctrine, which helped to shape the movement from a U.S. policy of friendship or détente toward the Soviet Union to one that focused largely upon the containment that was suggested in "The Sources of Soviet Conduct."

Two years following the article by Kennan the Soviet Union developed and tested a nuclear weapon in Kazakhstan. This test helped to launch a race for nuclear superiority between the Soviet Union and the United States that would last for much of the rest of the century. In November 1952, the United States tested its first thermonuclear device in the Marshall Islands; it yielded a blast much larger than the ones created at Hiroshima and Nagasaki. The power of the explosion created a crater one mile long and 175 feet deep (Newhouse 1989). Within nine months, the Soviet Union tested its first thermonuclear device. With each test, the Soviets or the United States sought to outdo the other in order to advance the extent and the limits of war.

In 1953, Robert Oppenheimer published a public version of a paper he had prepared for President Truman in the latter months of Truman's presidency. In the article, Oppenheimer suggested that the escalating American and Soviet arms race was similar to "two scorpions in a bottle, each capable of killing the other, but only at the risk of his own life" (Oppenheimer 1953, 529).

Despite the warnings from Oppenheimer and other scientists of the perils of what was becoming a pattern of nuclear escalation, President Eisenhower, who succeeded Truman as president of the United States, approved a policy document in 1953 known as NSC 162/2. This document argued that there were two primary interests in the formulation of nuclear weapon policies: addressing a perceived Soviet threat to U.S. security and ensuring that the United States was able to maintain a stable economic foundation while countering the perceived Soviet threat. As the report noted:

> The capability of the USSR to attack the United States with atomic weapons has been continuously growing and will be materially enhanced by hydrogen weapons. The USSR has sufficient bombs and aircraft, using one-way missions, to inflict serious damage on the United States, especially by surprise attack. The USSR soon may have the capacity of dealing a crippling blow to our industrial base and our continued ability to prosecute a war. Effective defense could reduce the likelihood and intensity of a hostile attack but not eliminate the chance of a crippling blow. (Lay 1953, 2)

The report later noted:

> With increasing atomic power, the Soviets have a mounting capability of inflicting very serious and possibly crippling damage on the United States. The USSR will also continue to have large military forces capable of aggressive action against the countries of the free world. Present estimates are, however, that the USSR will not deliberately initiate general war during the next several years, although general war might result from miscalculation. In the absence of general war, a prolonged period of tension may ensue, during which each side increases its armaments, reaches atomic plenty and seeks to improve its relative power position. (Lay 1953, 18)

The year following the release of NSC 162/2, Secretary of State John Foster Dulles presented a policy referred to as "massive retaliation," in which he said the administration had decided to "depend primarily upon a great capacity to retaliate, instantly, by means and places of our choosing" (Priest 2006, 9). The strength of the language and the notion of massive retaliation helped to further the process of escalation in both discourse and, ultimately, nuclear capabilities.

Despite the tone of these policies, Eisenhower maintained concerns about the ultimate path that might develop with continued nuclear activities. After the Soviet test of a hydrogen bomb in 1953, Eisenhower's concerns about mutual destruction in an era with nuclear capabilities became even greater.

As a result, in 1953, Eisenhower introduced an initiative that would help facilitate the development of peaceful uses of nuclear technology. He presented his plan for this strategy in early December 1953 at the United Nations in what became known as the Atoms for Peace speech. Eisenhower acknowledged that the U.S.'s stockpile of atomic weapons was growing to the extent that they had long since exceeded the explosive equivalent of all bombs and all shells used during World War II (Eisenhower 1953).

The year following Eisenhower's speech, the United States proposed to the United Nations the development of an international agency that would help control the flow of nuclear transactions. In 1957, the International Atomic Energy Agency (IAEA) was created to serve in this role. To date, the IAEA has engaged in working with the international community to ensure various protocols are in place to guarantee safe and peaceful use of nuclear technology.

THE COLD WAR: THE MIDDLE YEARS

Despite the strategies outlined in Eisenhower's Atoms for Peace speech to ensure the peaceful sharing of information about nuclear capabilities, the United States drafted its first plan for carrying out a nuclear war in the late 1950s. Known as the Single Integrated Operational Plan, it was based on the notion that if given adequate warning, the United States and its allies would launch their entire nuclear arsenal against the Soviet Union, China, and satellite states. According to George B. Kistiakowsky, Eisenhower's science adviser, after reviewing the plan, it would "lead to unnecessary and undesirable overkill" (Hoffman 2010, 16).

After learning details of the Single Integrated Operational Plan in 1961 following his inauguration, President Kennedy signaled his discomfort with the notion of massive retaliation by commenting to Secretary of State Dean Rusk, "and we call ourselves the human race" (Reeves 1994, 230). Kennedy's discomfort with the plan led him to revise the strategy to one referred to as "counterforce," which provided the president with more flexibility in waging a possible nuclear attack—with an aim of targeting largely Soviet weapons, not Soviet cities.

Robert McNamara, Kennedy's secretary of defense, realized that the limited counterforce would not strike every Soviet weapon. As a result, McNamara shifted to a strategy that he called "assured destruction," which required building the number of weapons needed to destroy 20–25 percent of the Soviet population and 50 percent of the industrial base. A central component of this strategy was to target military bases and outposts, not cities where sizable civilian populations would likely be casualties. Much of this strategy was based on a belief that the Soviet Union would exercise similar restraint.

The assumption of restraint was challenged with the Cuban Missile Crisis of 1962. When the crisis was over, McNamara was convinced that notions of restraint in the event of a nuclear war would not serve as an overall deterrent as much as the possibility of war that would ultimately result in the mutual destruction of as many civilians and members of the military as possible. This concept, which became known as Mutually Assured Destruction, placed cities and dense population areas as the center of the military targets. The specter of such wide-scale destruction did play a critical role in keeping the United States and the Soviet Union from a nuclear conflict for the remainder of the cold war.

The realization of the destruction that would result if the United States and the Soviet Union unleashed their nuclear arsenals upon one another led the nations to begin instituting a number of treaties with the goal of minimizing the nuclear threat. In 1963, the Limited Test Ban Treaty abolished nuclear tests in the atmosphere.

In 1968, the Nuclear Nonproliferation Treaty limited the ability of nuclear weapons–possessing nations to assist other nations in acquiring nuclear weapons. Two treaties were signed in 1972. First, the Strategic Arms Limitation Interim Agreement restricted the number of ballistic missiles that each side could have based on land or at sea. Second, the Anti-Ballistic Missile Treaty banned defenses against long-range missiles. The development of these treaties served as an indication that both sides were willing to build processes to ensure that nuclear conflict would not occur, the idea being that by achieving nuclear balance both nations would be able to ensure that the other would not begin a conflict.

By the late 1970s, it was believed within some policy circles that the Soviet Union was not concerned about parity in nuclear arsenals, but that it desired to build to a point of nuclear superiority. Paul Nitze, a former secretary of the navy, noted in an article in *Foreign Affairs* that the Soviets were not satisfied with parity or essential equivalence in nuclear weapons, but "will continue to pursue a nuclear superiority that is not merely quantitative but designed to produce a theoretical war-winning capability" (Nitze 1976, 207). This perspective became increasingly popular in policy circles, particularly in the aftermath of the 1980 presidential elections and the advent of the Reagan administration.

The 1980s witnessed a dramatic shift in U.S.-Soviet relations. We began the decade with continued escalation of nuclear capabilities in each nation, both able to destroy one another. By 1985, the United States had nearly doubled the Pentagon's budget. Much of the thinking of the Reagan administration was that by increasing the military's budget and negotiating for arms reduction strategies, we would ultimately witness a reduction or elimination of nuclear arms.

A critical element of the U.S. strategy was the development of the Strategic Defense Initiative (SDI)—a missile defense shield that would be partially based in space. This approach to developing a greater protection system for the United States also served as a major obstacle in advancing further nuclear weapons treaties.

In 1986, the explosion at the Chernobyl nuclear plant (see next chapter) caused Mikhail Gorbachev, then the general secretary of the Communist Party of the USSR, to rethink the direction of USSR policy. He later condemned the secrecy of the Soviet system and call for policies of glasnost (openness) and perestroika (restructuring) in the Soviet Union (Gorbachev 1996, 191–93).

He carried this perspective to the 1986 summit with Ronald Reagan in Reykjavik, Iceland. At the meeting, Gorbachev proposed a 50 percent reduction in Soviet and American strategic weapons, with the United States continuing to honor the Anti-Ballistic Missile Treaty (which the Soviets viewed the SDI initiative as violating). Reagan countered with a goal of phasing out all international ballistic missiles and an offer to share the SDI. Neither was able to convince the other of a deal.

A few years after the meeting at Reykjavik, rapid change was under way in Europe. The Soviet Union was beginning its process of breaking up. The Berlin Wall was being torn down, a sign of movement toward the reunification of Germany. Other nations in the former Eastern Bloc would soon implement strategies for economic and political reform. The end of this Eastern Bloc, and the Soviet Union as the power guiding much of it, would leave a number of pressing questions concerning nuclear safety from a military viewpoint.

POST–COLD WAR NUCLEAR THREATS

The years since the cold war have been shaped by military concerns over the possibility of a post–cold war nuclear crisis. The first concern arose in the early 1990s and focused on how to address the issue of nuclear stockpiles in many of the former Soviet regions. At the close of the cold war, it was estimated that there were over twenty thousand tactical warheads in the newly independent states. Many of these warheads were aimed at the United States, and their ownership and control were ambiguous. As a result, one of the initial challenges in the immediate post–cold war era was to bring many of these arms under stable control or rapid decommission.

The second concern was how to balance the challenges of a world with new nuclear states. When the agreement that established the IAEA was formulated in the late 1950s, a handful of nations had developed nuclear weapons. Now there are many more. With regional tensions still a large part of the global landscape, one of the concerns is whether nuclear weapons might be used in a relatively small regional conflict. A primary area of concern is in South Asia, where India and Pakistan, nations that have had significantly tense relations for many years, have both acquired nuclear capabilities. Other nations of concern regarding their quest to obtain nuclear weapons include North Korea and Iran. How can we ensure that these nations, newly armed with nuclear weapons, restrain from engaging in nuclear conflict?

The third concern focuses on how to prevent members of terrorist organizations from obtaining nuclear weapons. In some of the nations that do have such weapons, how secure are their nuclear assets? The possibility that an organization such as Al Qaeda could obtain a nuclear weapon is clearly a threat that a nuclear-enabled world must consider. If these assets are not secure and a terrorist organization is able to obtain a weapon, the possibilities of nuclear disaster would be greatly enhanced.

CONCLUSION

In his 1969 book *Present at the Creation*, former U.S. secretary of state Dean Acheson reflects on his own realizations and those of others who were involved in shaping U.S. foreign policy in the early years of the nuclear era. "Only slowly did it dawn upon us that the whole world structure and the order we had inherited was gone," he writes (Acheson 1987, 726). The actions of Acheson and many of the other decision makers engaged in the developments of the era did help to fuel a world where nuclear use of weapons for belligerent purposes would forever be a possibility.

The new world structure has moved beyond a reality of a handful of nations with nuclear capabilities to a reality where the number of nations with such capabilities is far more extensive than Acheson and his colleagues imagined.

Luckily, the wisdom of many of the individuals guiding public policies during the cold war and thus far in this post–cold war era have prevented the leaders controlling nuclear weapons from unwisely using the nuclear weapons available. Thus far, despite the presence of nuclear weapons in our world, we have not seen them used since the middle of the 1940s.

11

Balancing the Optimism and Risks of Civilian Nuclear Energy

"It is not too much to expect that our children will enjoy in their homes electrical energy too cheap to meter," declared Lewis Strauss, chairman of the U.S. Atomic Energy Commission in a speech to the National Association of Science Writers in 1954 (Smith 2007, 3). For Strauss, the nuclear era that the world had recently entered was framed by a perspective that energy would be both inexpensive and accessible to a larger segment of the population than ever before. While quick to consider the seemingly limitless possibilities of a nuclear era, Strauss and many of his colleagues promoting civilian nuclear power were either not cognizant of, or simply ignored, many of the risks that might emerge with such capabilities.

Certainly he and others engaged in policy making in the mid-twentieth century were aware of nuclear energy's destructive capabilities, particularly in the aftermath of the bombing of Hiroshima and Nagasaki just a few years earlier. But Strauss and many of his colleagues anticipated that the advancement of nuclear capabilities would develop into the means to use such technologies to provide energy in the United States and elsewhere.

While the opportunities for inexpensive energy production were seemingly limitless, agency officials, industrial leaders, and others were beginning to actively address questions focused on the safety of nuclear energy production. If there were to be some type of accident at a nuclear facility, many wondered, who would be responsible? Were there any effective means, particularly given the risks of nuclear energy production, to ensure the safety of people working in or situated near such facilities?

This chapter examines many of the questions regarding the opportunity and risk that coincide with the emergence of nuclear energy for civilian use. I begin with an examination of legislative acts that facilitated the infrastructure to develop civilian nuclear energy, with an emphasis on three initial acts: the 1946 Atomic Energy Act, the 1954 Atomic Energy Act, and the 1957 Price-Anderson Act. I then examine a series of crises that occurred with the development of civilian nuclear energy.

Each crisis has given reasons for policy makers and the general public to weigh the benefits and costs of civilian nuclear energy. I close the chapter with a reexamination of several of these questions in light of the continued use of civilian nuclear energy despite the risks that became a reality in these disasters.

NUCLEAR POTENTIAL ACKNOWLEDGED

The end of World War II left U.S. policy makers with the knowledge that the nation had the ability to leverage an immense amount of energy in the wake of the theories, research, and development that we had tested in Hiroshima and Nagasaki. The development of these nuclear technologies left the nation with an infrastructure that could advance future nuclear capabilities. However, it also left a number of questions about using these new materials for peaceful purposes.

Central among these questions was the issue of safety. While many advocates wanted to maximize the benefits of this new energy, few people were willing to speak of its risks. In some cases, this unwillingness was from a lack of awareness of the potential dangers; in other cases, it was due to a sense of optimism that kept advocates for nuclear energy focused on its possibilities.

In 1946, the Atomic Energy Act was introduced to control postwar nuclear systems. In its original form, the act called for the military to continue its oversight and control of nuclear power during the postwar era. Many scientists were concerned about the potential abuse of power if the military retained control over nuclear capabilities. The lobbying by members of the scientific community and tensions between President Truman and the officers in the War Department ultimately led Truman to support a bill to establish a civilian-based nuclear commission: the Atomic Energy Commission.

By the 1950s, the Atomic Energy Commission's promotion of civilian nuclear energy was gaining an increasing number of supporters. There was a great deal of enthusiasm regarding the possibilities of civilian nuclear energy production. In 1952, Gordon Dean, chairman of the Atomic Energy Commission, claimed in a speech before the American Bar Association:

> In many ways we are at a crossroads in the peaceful development of atomic energy. . . . I say we are at a crossroads because of the many lines of development which are reaching crucial points almost simultaneously—such as the interest of the military in mobile reactors to power submarines, ships and aircraft; the interest of the industry in the production of central station power concurrently with plutonium; the interests of the scientists in the development of small nuclear power plants; and the intensification of the interest of industry, agriculture, medicine and science in the utilization of radioisotopes . . . we are going to push forward in this field of peaceful uses. . . . And in doing so we are inevitably going to push into an area where a whole range of questions of basic public policy must be faced up to and resolved. . . . Most of these questions revolve around the central fact that today atomic energy in this country is a 100-percent government monopoly, and it is a monopoly because that is the law of the land. But if the peaceful uses of atomic energy are to be brought to full flower, and find a permanent and secure home in our economy, is it not true that the government must relinquish at least part of its monopoly? We think it is. (Dean 1952)

Dean's address to the bar association was part of a larger campaign to build support for a new piece of legislation supporting nuclear exchange. Ultimately, through what would become the 1954 Atomic Energy Act, the government was indicating its desire to demonstrate that private industry could begin to engage further in the development of the field of civilian nuclear energy production.

Despite the passage of the 1954 act, the private sector was still apprehensive about civilian nuclear power. While companies acknowledged the profit potential of nuclear energy production, many also recognized the risks associated with it. The potential costs of an accident were seemingly limitless, and few private companies were willing to risk those costs. Without clarification of responsibility for what could be an expensive proposition, few companies were willing to seriously explore business opportunities in the nuclear arena without a means of minimizing the potential liability.

In response to these concerns, Congress passed the Price-Anderson Act in 1957. Price-Anderson removed a major economic barrier to the development of civilian nuclear power by establishing a $560 million limit on a utility's liability for a nuclear accident. This legislation encouraging companies to proceed played an important role in the development of an infrastructure for civilian nuclear energy production.

In the same year as the passage of the Price-Anderson Act, the Brookhaven National Laboratory completed a report requested by the Atomic Energy Commission on a possible emergency scenario at a hypothetical nuclear power plant. "Theoretical Possibilities and Consequences of Major Accidents in Large Nuclear Power Plants," commonly known as the "WASH 740" report, provided estimates of fatality rates and other harm that might emerge from an accident at a nuclear facility.

Of the several risks presented in WASH 740, the most serious threat to the larger public would be contamination from the release of radioactive fission products stored in the hypothetical reactor. It was estimated that such an accident would result in the airborne dispersal of radioactive material over a wide area. According to the report, such exposure could lead to the deaths of 3,400 people and 43,000 injuries within a range of roughly forty-five miles.

Despite this scenario, the report's authors repeated the belief shared by the majority of scientists involved in the research—the chances of such occurrences happening were exceedingly low. With the report came a letter of transmittal to Congress from Harold Vance, then chairman of the Atomic Energy Commission, which stated that many of the experts who developed the report agreed that the chances of a major accident were minimal:

> Nuclear reactors have been operated since December 2, 1942, with a safety record far better than that of even the safest industry. More

than 100 reactor years of regular operating experience have been accumulated, including experience with reactors of high power and large inventories of fission products, without a single personal injury and no significant deposition of radioactivity outside of the plant area. There have been a few accidents with experimental reactor installations as contrasted with the perfect record of safety of the regularly operating reactors. But even these accidents did not affect the public. (U.S. Atomic Energy Commission 1957, vii)

At the same time that the WASH 740 report was being written, researchers at the University of Michigan were considering the potential risks at the proposed Enrico Fermi reactor, which was about to be built at Michigan's Lagoona Beach. As in WASH 740, one of the concerns noted in the University Michigan report was the potential for the release of fission material into the air.

Unlike the hypothetical reactor in the WASH 740 report, however, the Fermi reactor would be a real one with real population centers nearby. One of the population centers near Fermi was Detroit, a mere thirty miles away from the site. The University of Michigan report suggested that if a radiation plume reached Detroit, thousands of people would be exposed to near lethal levels of radiation, and an additional 180,000 people would receive a level that would triple their chances of getting leukemia or other forms of cancer within ten years (Gomberg 1957, 62).

NUCLEAR RISKS REALIZED

Early in the morning of October 5, 1966, nine years after the University of Michigan's risk analysis on the Fermi plant had presented its scenario of a nuclear crisis for Detroit and other cities, an alarm went off in one of the site's containment buildings. Several indicators of high levels of radiation from the initial melting of fuel at the reactor were detected. Engineers raced to the accident to ensure that there was no leak of radiation. A breach of radiation containment with the right wind speed and wind direction would, as the report suggested, have sent radioactive fallout over Detroit. Luckily, such a worst-case scenario didn't occur, and the accident was contained before it escalated into the catastrophe described in the University of Michigan's analysis. However, it did provide evidence that, despite assurances by scientists and policy makers, accidents could occur at nuclear reactors.

Two years after the incident at the Fermi reactor, the assumptions of safety would take a step closer to being tested again when the Atomic Energy Commission gave provisional authorization to the Metropolitan Edison Company to build a nuclear facility at Three Mile Island, near Harrisburg, Pennsylvania.

NUCLEAR SAFETY IN THE 1970s

In 1975, nine years after the Fermi incident, Congress created the Nuclear Regulatory Commission (NRC) to assume many of the responsibilities of the Atomic Energy Commission. For some time preceding the creation of the NRC, the Atomic Energy Commission's regulatory programs had been under attack by Congress, which was particularly concerned that the AEC had two opposing yet equally important roles. The first role was as an organization tasked with promoting the commercial use of nuclear energy. The second was the regulation of such energy. The concern was that an agency tasked with both promoting the use of nuclear energy and regulating the nuclear energy field would be facing conflicting goals.

In October 1975, the Nuclear Regulatory Commission released a study by Norman Rasmussen, a professor in the Department of Nuclear Engineering at the Massachusetts Institute of Technology, on the potential risks of an accident at any of the existing nuclear power plants across the nation. Like the WASH 740 report and the University of Michigan Report on the Fermi reactor, the Rasmussen Report indicated that the potential of risk at one of the existing reactors was minimal:

> The likelihood of reactor accidents is much smaller than that of many non-nuclear accidents having similar consequences. All non-nuclear accidents examined in this study, including fires, explosions, toxic chemical releases, dam failures, airplane crashes, earthquakes, hurricanes, and tornadoes, are much more likely to occur and can have consequences comparable to, or larger than, those of nuclear accidents. (Rasmussen 1974, 1)

While the report indicated that a nuclear accident was unlikely, it did provide an overview of the types of accidents that could occur. One of the largest concerns was the release of radioactivity from a core meltdown. However, the report indicated that the chance of such a meltdown occurring before 1980, six years from the date of the report's initial release, was one in 200 per year, a very unlikely possibility.

In September 1974, a year before the release of the Rasmussen report, Metropolitan Edison began operating the first of its two units at Three Mile Island. The second reactor unit opened four years later, in December 1978. Both units at Three Mile Island used nuclear fission to produce heat that converted water to steam, which in turn powered turbines that produced electricity.

Early in the morning of Wednesday, March 28, 1979, while undergoing routine maintenance, the pump that fed water into the main system of Three Mile Island's second reactor unit stopped functioning, resulting in the shutdown of the turbines and ultimately the reactor. By 7 a.m. that morning, rising temperatures within an already deteriorating core prompted officials to declare a site emergency. By 7:30, a general emergency had been declared, and local and state officials began weighing evacuation protocols in the area to prevent widespread harm.

For several days, scientists and engineers involved with Three Mile Island were unclear about the impact of the accident. They were unsure how much radiation was leaking into the larger community and what the impact of such a radiation leak would be.

By Friday, experts realized that the sudden increase in pressure that had taken place on Wednesday was actually a hydrogen explosion. Though the explosion was large enough to destroy a small building, it was contained in the 600,000-cubic-foot structure surrounded by four-foot-thick concrete walls.

POSTDISASTER ASSESSMENT

In October 1979 a report by the President's Commission on the Accident at Three Mile Island identified the balance between human error and the technical failures that resulted in the accident. The report outlined broad systemic challenges in the manufacture, operation, and regulation of nuclear power, as well as pointing out various structural challenges around the individual organizations engaged in the nuclear field. The report observed that the safety record of nuclear power plants had supported the assumption, and conviction, that these plants, including Three Mile Island, were safe:

> After many years of operation of nuclear power plants, with no evidence that any member of the general public has been hurt, the belief that nuclear power plants are sufficiently safe grew into a conviction. The Commission is convinced that this attitude must be changed to one that says nuclear power is by its very nature potentially dangerous, and therefore, one must continually question whether the safeguards already in place are sufficient to prevent major accidents. (Kemeny 1979, 9)

Finally, the report noted that the multitude of factors that resulted in the occurrence at Three Mile Island went beyond merely inappropriate action by the operator, but extended as far back as the broader regulatory oversight over this industry. It concluded:

> . . . while the major factor that turned this incident into a serious accident was inappropriate operator action, many factors contributed to the action of the operators, such as deficiencies in their training, lack of clarity in their operating procedures, failure of organizations to learn the proper lessons from previous incidents, and deficiencies in the design of the control room. These shortcomings are attributable to the utility, to suppliers of equipment, and to the federal commission that regulates nuclear power. Therefore—whether or not operator error "explains" this particular case—given all the above deficiencies, we are convinced that an accident like Three Mile Island was eventually inevitable. (Kemeny 1979, 11)

Much of the story of Three Mile Island is the nuclear catastrophe that could have been but luckily was averted. Five years after the release of the report, in July 1984, the reactor head of Three Mile Island was lifted to lower cameras to photograph the internal rubble. The footage retrieved demonstrated that at some point on the morning of March 28, 1979, the plant was within thirty minutes of a full nuclear meltdown.

NUCLEAR CIVILIAN ISSUES:
INTERNATIONAL QUESTIONS

On Monday, April 28, 1986, sensors at a nuclear plant in Sweden detected a 150-fold increase in the level of radiation in the air. Shortly afterward, other power stations in northern Europe reported similar readings. By early Monday afternoon, Sweden's national Defense Research Institute had analyzed weather patterns and identified the source of the radiation as somewhere in the Ukraine. By Monday evening, Sweden had pinpointed the source as Chernobyl, a town with a nuclear facility in the Soviet Union.

On April 26, 1986, two days before radioactivity was detected in Sweden, a test was performed at the V.I. Lenin Power Station in Chernobyl. An operator at the nuclear plant moved the control rods of one of the reactors to slightly below the correct position and inadvertently released a plume containing millions of curies of deadly radioactive aerosol into the air. It moved toward the north and the west and within a few days had reached nearly every country in the northern hemisphere.

A number of health issues arose in the years following Chernobyl. More than 5 million people lived in areas that were classified as contaminated; roughly 400,000 people lived in the most contaminated areas. In the years immediately following the incident at Chernobyl, approximately 350,000 people were relocated away from the contaminated areas.

Chernobyl gave rise to many questions about the management of nuclear facilities. A central question was what kind of controls were in place to ensure the safe use of nuclear power, and what recourse is there when a nuclear power mishap occurs in one country but moves into another.

Chernobyl served as the catalyst for a critical discussion under the auspices of the International Atomic Energy Association (IAEA) on the international dimensions of nuclear safety, particularly how the international community might respond to the Chernobyl crisis. In September 1986, the IAEA adopted the Convention on Early Notification and Accidents, to ensure that nations were notified in the event of a nuclear emergency that could stretch across national borders. At the same general conference, the IAEA adopted the Convention on Assistance in the Case of a Nuclear Accident or Radiological Emergency (the Assistance Convention), establishing a framework for the development of emergency assistance between signatories in the event of a nuclear emergency.

Eight years later, in June 1994, the Convention on Nuclear Safety (CNS) was adopted. The CNS requires states to fulfill a number of obligations relating to the regulation, management, and operation of nuclear power plants. It was also partially an attempt to ensure that all countries that have nuclear energy as a source of power abide by certain standards that minimize accidents, particularly those that have cross-border implications.

CONCLUSIONS

Twenty-five years after Chernobyl, an earthquake and tsunami triggered a nuclear leak at the Fukushima nuclear facility in Japan. The sequence of events was initiated by an earthquake of 9.0 magnitude off the Japanese coast. The quake triggered tsunamis that struck several coastal cities in northeastern Japan, including the locale of the Fukushima plant. The crisis demonstrated that the risks of nuclear energy production include natural disasters such as earthquakes and tsunamis. The accident affirmed that those involved with risk analyses in the field of nuclear energy development must take into account the possibility of broader accidents not originating at the plants. In the case of the Fukushima disaster, postaccident questions were raised about the risk of having nuclear plants in countries such as Japan that have a high amount of seismic activity.

Japan's challenge as it weighs the lessons of Fukushima is similar to that of other nations weighing the costs and benefits of nuclear energy. The world's overall demand for energy will expand over time—a demand felt on regional and local levels. Nuclear energy—if safely generated—can produce inexpensive power with a much lower greenhouse effect than other forms of energy production.

How to generate sufficient energy to meet this demand—and whether, given all of the risks, nuclear energy will be the ideal source of power production—will be one of the pressing questions that policy makers will have to face over the next several decades.

12

Hazardous Waste

When children in the neighborhood surrounding the 99th Street School in Niagara Falls, NY, began to complain of itchiness in the 1970s, many of the local residents failed to make an immediate connection between their complaints and the odors that were coming from their basements. But in time, the appearance of skin lesions and burns, and eventually of material seeping from the ground, provided enough reason for people to begin asking questions about what was happening in their neighborhood.

For many of the residents, the name William Love was unfamiliar. His ambitions, however, provided a component of the answers to the questions they found themselves asking about their community. In the late 1800s, after Love's dream of building a canal as part of a model city in the region failed, he abandoned the land he had acquired for the project, including the partially dug canal. A few years later, the land with the canal was transferred to the Hooker Chemical and Plant Company, which made various bleaches and caustic soda. The Hooker Company then used the unfinished canal as a dumping ground for over twenty thousand tons of hazardous chemical waste during the 1940s and early 1950s. In 1953, the company sold the majority of the land to the local school district, and ultimately it became the site of the 99th Street School and the homes surrounding it.

Within a few years, various health issues began surfacing in the community. People began noticing rashes, children were getting ill, and there were seemingly high rates of cancer and miscarriage. In time, these health concerns would lead to the development of legislation at the federal and state levels for cleaning up toxic wastes and holding responsible parties liable for environmental harm.

The environmental crisis of the Love Canal represented a shift in acknowledgment of the risks that come with the waste generated by industrial activities. After years of creating wastes as a by-product of the industrial advances in the late-nineteenth and the twentieth centuries, people were beginning to ask critical questions about their disposal. The recognition of the problem at a community level spurred action toward a higher level by mobilizing politicians and others to address the problem of hazardous waste. Ultimately, crises caused businesses, policy makers, and others to recognize that the various items we could create in a modern industrial era carried with them serious environmental and public health challenges.

WILLIAM LOVE'S DREAM

William Love's dream for the area that eventually became best known as the Love Canal emerged with the opportunity that he saw to link the upper and lower sections of the Niagara River. His plan called for using the new canal not only as a means of improving transportation in the region but also to provide a source of power generation for the industries that he hoped would become situated by the canal. At the time, it was important for industries to be located near their sources of power—and for Love, the notion of an industrial base being developed near the power source of the canal provided an opportunity for new community and industrial development initiatives.

Love, however, had not anticipated two factors that would ultimately destroy his dreams of a model city by the canal. First, the economic depression of the 1890s would limit his ability to secure financing for the project. Initial financiers who had committed early funding simply were not able to follow through because of the depression. Second, advances brought about by Tesla's invention that enabled electricity to be transmitted across great distances diminished the need to locate industry next to sources of electrical power. Thus, part of the justification for the location of the canal project, as a generator of power for local industry, had limited value. As a result, Love was forced to close the company established for building his canal and model city. In 1897, he abandoned his partially dug canal, and in 1927, the city of Niagara Falls annexed it.

At roughly the same time that Love was realizing that the dreams of his planned community would not be fulfilled, the foundations for the rapid expansion of the chemical industry in the United States were beginning to develop. Many companies were coming up with new processes for creating the chemicals that would play a critical role in newly developing industries. Many of these had to face a challenge: how to dispose of the thousands of gallons of chemical by-product left from the manufacture of these new products. In an era that did not have the environmental awareness to which we are now accustomed, any place where chemicals could be dumped proved to be the answer.

During World War II, Hooker Chemicals was one of scores of companies that profited from the war's needs for products made with chemicals. Many of the products and materials that Hooker developed for both its military and its civilian customers had numerous chemical by-products. The company needed locations to discard them. In 1942, William Love's former canal was purchased by the Hooker Chemical Company for this very purpose.

From the time of its acquisition of the canal until 1953, Hooker deposited chemical waste onto the property. Drums of waste were covered with clay and soil. At times, the drums caved in, and so the waste mixed with the soil or clay meant to cover the drums.

Management at Hooker was aware of the potential risks but continued to deposit the chemical waste in the canal. In 1944, Hooker's Annual Operations Report stated that burying its residues was "creating a potential future hazard" and predicted that continuing to do so "will be a potential source of law suits in the future" (Hernan 2010, 63). In 1946, Ansley Wilcox II, Hooker's general counsel, visited the site and wrote a memorandum to the president of the company in which he expressed several of his concerns. He noted:

> . . . the entire length of the canal is filled with water and to my in-
> experienced eye it seemed clear that the water was contaminated.
> I understand that children in the neighborhood use portions of the

water for swimming and, as a matter of fact, just before we left the site we saw several young children walking down the path with what appeared to be bathing costumes in hand. . . . I feel very strongly that if this water is contaminated as a result of our dumping chemical residues we are running a real hazard in not taking steps to prevent possible injuries to persons who may swim in the canal. (*United States v. Hooker Chemicals & Plastics Corp.*, 1019)

In October 1950, a representative of Hooker reported to management that the ash being dumped into the canal was blowing toward houses east of the canal. He also observed that the water in the canal was contaminated by an oil slick and that the "ground had settled enough to open pot holes of various depths and that portions of buried drums were exposed in these holes." The representative reportedly told management that "it is felt that a fence around this property would be very desirable from a safety standpoint" (Hernan 2010, 64).

In the spring of 1952, the Niagara Falls school board asked if Hooker would consider selling a part of the Love Canal property for the site of a school that the city was looking to build. Initially, due largely to its awareness of the chemical waste it had been depositing in the area, Hooker hesitated in following up with the school district's inquiry. Within a few weeks, however, the company decided to move forward with the transfer. As one of the managers responsible for the decision wrote at the time:

The more we thought about it, the more interested . . . [we] became in the proposition and finally came to the conclusion that the Love Canal property is rapidly becoming a liability . . . [we] became convinced that it would be a wise move to turn the property over to the schools provided we would not be held responsible for future claims or damages resulting from underground storage of chemicals. (*United States v. Hooker Chemicals & Plastics Corp.*, 1016)

Within several weeks of the school board's initial inquiry, the company sold the sixteen-acre property to the Board of Education of the City of Niagara Falls for $1.00 for use as an elementary school. A central component of the deed was a provision that protected the company from liability should any problem arise from the chemicals deposited there.

RISING ENVIRONMENTAL AWARENESS

During the 1960s an increasing awareness was emerging of the environmental harm that was being caused by various industrial activities. These incidents led to the development of new approaches for identifying and managing environmental risks. In 1969, the National Environmental and Policy Act was passed by Congress and signed into law by President Nixon. Three years later, the 1972 Clean Water Act was passed and also signed into law. These pieces of legislation indicated a broadening awareness of environmental concerns stemming from rapid industrialization. The nation was becoming concerned about the short- and long-term impact of environmental waste on people and their communities.

LOVE CANAL: THE CRISIS EMERGES

"When we moved into our house on 101st Street in 1972, I didn't even know Love Canal was there," wrote Louise Gibbs, who lived with her family in one of the homes surrounding the 99th Street School. "It was a lovely neighborhood in a quiet residential area, with lots of trees and lots of children outside playing. It seemed just the place for our family" (Gibbs 1998, 9).

But Gibbs would soon enough find out about the history of the area and the harm that it would bring to her family and scores of other families in the area. There had been reports over the years of various chemicals and of sludge appearing in parts of the community. As far back as 1955, shortly after the 99th Street School had opened, roughly twenty-five square feet of ground crumbled near the original excavation, exposing the drums and chemicals. Some of the children were splashed and their eyes were burned. The school principal called Hooker Chemicals to ask for information about the chemicals, and a Hooker representative was sent to investigate, along with the Hooker plant nurse. The nurse provided advice on appropriate first aid, and Hooker arranged for ten trucks of dirt and a bulldozer to cover and grade the exposed area.

Gibbs's concerns arose when one of her children began having seizures and the school district would not let her change schools for him. Research initially meant to convince the school district to reconsider its decisions led her to discover numerous health issues that were surfacing with other residents in the area.

For a number of years, many of the people in the community ignored many of these incidents. However, reports began to circulate in the 1970s about health conditions that were appearing with worrisome frequency among residents in the area surrounding the 99th Street School. In 1978 it was reported that a large number of the children were born with significant birth defects—thus warranting further investigation. In other cases, it became apparent that other health challenges were related to the conditions in and around the canal.

In the fall of 1977 the state requested the assistance of the Environmental Protection Agency (EPA) to conduct further studies of the subsurface conditions and to monitor the air in the basements of homes adjacent to the canal. The EPA representative who inspected the site found conditions to be not only unhealthy and hazardous, but unprecedented in scope.

On August 2, 1978, the New York State Department of Health (DOH) recommended relocating all pregnant women and children under the age of two due to health concerns caused by the toxins. Later that month, President Carter declared the environmental crisis at Love Canal to be a federal emergency. With the assistance of state and federal resources, families from the areas surrounding the school were relocated. As Carter noted:

> Last May, because of concern about the potential health effects from exposure to chemical wastes, I declared an emergency for the Love Canal neighborhood and authorized relocation of about 700 families to temporary quarters. At the same time, I committed Federal resources to conduct further health and environmental studies in the area. This appropriation request will make available funds for the Centers for Disease Control in conjunction with the State University of New York at Buffalo, to carry out my commitment to residents of the area. (Carter 1980)

Federal funds were committed to assisting the state in the relocation process, and the state government agreed to permanently relocate people living on both sides of the streets adjacent to the canal and to buy their homes. In total, with the assistance of state and federal resources, over two hundred families were evacuated from Love Canal that year.

In 1980, the results of blood tests from the residents were released. When these results showed chromosomal damage, a sign of certain cancers, and birth and other genetic disorders, President Carter declared a second state of emergency for the area on October 1, 1980. Almost nine hundred families evacuated Love Canal after these findings.

TOXIC WASTES: THE LARGER PICTURE

Love Canal came at a point when there was growing concern regarding toxic wastes in communities across the nation. It was, however, only one of a number of incidents that raised awareness of environmental and public health concerns that stemmed from years of reckless disposal of industrial waste. In Times Beach, Missouri, for example, high levels of dioxin detected in soil samples led the federal government to purchase the homes and businesses there and relocate residents.

Partially as a result of the Love Canal disaster, as well as other environmental crises of the late 1970s, the Comprehensive Environmental Response, Compensation, and Liability Act (CERCLA) was enacted on December 11, 1980. The act, commonly referred to as the Superfund Act, taxed petroleum and chemical industries to create a fund for any necessary cleanups of hazardous waste. CERCLA established prohibitions and requirements aimed at closed and abandoned hazardous waste sites; provided for liability of persons responsible for release of hazardous waste at these sites; and established a trust fund to pay for cleanup when no responsible party could be identified.

States followed with their own policies to handle cleanup measures around toxic wastes that were largely the result of industrial activities and the development of chemical products. These state policies required states to assess the exposure of their residents to potential health risks as well as harm done to the greater environment.

CONCLUSION

The crisis of Love Canal shows the risks that emerged with the development of industrial waste and strategies used over the years to dispose of the waste.

It also signified the beginning of an era when the public and policy makers more fully understood the consequences of long-term and wide distribution of wastes from chemical production or other means. In the years following the Love Canal crisis, numerous attempts would be made to implement institutional mechanisms for effectively handling industrial waste and ironing out the challenges that it created for society.

One of the long-term effects of the enhanced regulations for the disposal of waste was that many corporations increasingly looked to move their production and disposal facilities to other nations where the controls and regulations would not be as stringent as those in the United States. In due time, questions about the risk of moving the production and disposal offshore as a strategy for avoiding such regulation would surface as companies would find themselves having to contend with a future set of environmental crises.

13

Industrial Accidents and Determining Liability

Bhopal

For the people living in the informal settlements adjacent to the new Union Carbide facility in Bhopal, India, there were a number of hopes tied to the plant's presence. Many saw the prospect of employment, even in the most menial of jobs, as a clear benefit. Several of the people living in the camps realized that the plant was making pesticides that would ultimately increase the production of crops, yielding more food for a population that was struggling with the challenges of food production.

In December 1984, the excitement came to a standstill when a large quantity of methyl isocyanate gas (MIC) escaped from the plant. Carried by a breeze, the gas eventually made its way from the plant into the adjacent homes of the town's residents. Within a few hours, corpses were littering the streets. Of the more than 200,000 people exposed to the gas, it was estimated that over 2,500 men, women, and children died within the first week, mostly within the neighborhoods closest to the plant. In 1989, the death toll was estimated at 3,598, and by 1994, that number increased to more than 6,000.

The incident at Bhopal speaks to two critical issues in our exploration of late-modern risks and disaster. First is the story of the event. With over 6,000 deaths attributed to the accident and thousands more injuries, Bhopal is an example of the broader harm that can result from an industrial disaster. Production of chemical products, as Bhopal demonstrated, involves risks and raises questions about public safety near the manufacturing of harmful compounds.

Second is the complexity of identifying responsible parties and building a sense of accountability after a major industrial accident.

The Union Carbide plant in Bhopal was a joint venture with several stakeholders, including Union Carbide in the United States and the Indian government. Both India and the United States have their distinct court systems, which makes addressing matters of jurisdiction a critical and complex matter. The various stakeholders, ranging from multiple governments to the poor dwellers near the Union Carbide plant to officials from Union Carbide, represent a wide range of interests in finding someone to hold accountable for the accident at Union Carbide. The question of liability in an international crisis such as this was a difficult challenge.

I begin this examination of the Bhopal crisis with a look at the initial arrival of Union Carbide in India and the development of the Bhopal plant. I continue with an overview of the accident. Next, I examine legal questions from the aftermath. I close the chapter with a brief exploration of Bhopal's impact on a broader set of issues regarding industrial accidents and risk, particularly in an era when the interrelations between institutions that have a role in creating the risk may be far more complex than previously imagined.

UNION CARBIDE COMES TO INDIA

Union Carbide and India had been developing a special relationship over a number of years. For at least a decade, beginning in the 1960s, batteries manufactured by the company were used in lamps the company also provided to people in rural areas of India. The company increasingly provided insecticides that helped India enhance its agricultural productivity in what was referred to as the green revolution in agriculture, an effort that was perceived as increasing access to food for millions of people in impoverished nations around the world. Over time, people began to view the company as one that helped to provide some of the conveniences that they were hearing people in other nations had long been able to access.

Increasing environmental regulations of the 1960s and 1970s in the United States led many companies to seek other nations with fewer restrictions in which to engage in production. While standards were increasing in the United States, other nations were excited to have the increased capability to produce and sell items domestically and to the world. India was one of the nations that welcomed the new level of production. In 1977, Union Carbide opened a plant in Bhopal, India, to manufacture Sevin, a common pesticide (Fortun 2001, 259).

India provided an opportunity for Union Carbide to produce pesticides in an area with fewer regulations than in the United States, as well as proximity to a market for the pesticides it produced. The presence of its plant seemed to be a winning proposition for several stakeholders. Union Carbide received a way to make its products in a less expensive and less constraining regulatory environment. India received a foreign investor. The people of the Bhopal area were given hundreds of new jobs.

The new plant was to be a partnership between the government of India and Union Carbide. Union Carbide owned 50.9 percent of the company established in India, the government owned 22 percent, and private investors owned the remaining percentage.

THE ACCIDENT

On the night of December 2, 1984, a toxic gas known as methyl isocyanate began to leak from one of its containers at the Bhopal plant and drift across the city. Many of the people living in a squatter encampment next to the plant detected the leak almost immediately.

"As soon as my husband opened the door, all we could see was smoke entering our house," said Puna Bai, then a young mother of three living in one of the informal settlements near the factory. "Then everyone in my family started coughing and my kids started complaining of their eyes burning. Then we heard someone saying that we should all run because some gas pipe has exploded in the Union Carbide factory. We all started running and eventually I got separated from my family. I just remember not being able to locate my family and then after that I had lost consciousness" (Christianson 2010, 104).

Puna Bai was among the thousands of victims of the MIC gas leak at Bhopal, on record as being been one of the worst industrial accidents in the world.

The leak was the result of the failure of two key safety measures that had been dismantled several weeks prior to the accident, including turning off a device meant to neutralize toxic discharge. Without these two measures in place, pressure and heat from the reaction between the MIC and water in the plant continued to build.

In reports shortly after the leak, a number of causes were identified. A *New York Times* investigation pointed to a combination of minimal oversight, poor management, and technological failure as factors leading to the accident. Ten years later, another report suggested that the leak was the result of worker sabotage. In the case of either of these causes or others that were speculated, several thousand people were dead and several thousand more were injured.

THE CASE/LITIGATION

A central lesson that emerged from the Bhopal incident centered on how legal systems might respond to a crisis of this magnitude and that stretched across national borders. Immediately following the gas leak, a number of attorneys from the United States went to India in an attempt to identify possible claimants against Union Carbide. On December 7, 1984, just a few days after the leak, a lawsuit was filed against Union Carbide in Institute, West Virginia, where the company had another plant. Within months there were dozens of additional suits. By the end of December 1984, the Indian government was threatening to file a suit in the United States against the company on behalf of all Indian victims.

In March 1985, the Indian government passed the Bhopal Gas Leak Disaster Act. The act gave the Indian government the exclusive right to represent everyone who made a claim or intended to make a claim against Union Carbide for injuries resulting from the accident at Bhopal and to coordinate the five hundred claims that had been filed by then in India. On April 8, 1985, India brought its suit against Union Carbide in the U.S. District Court in the Southern District of New York. The Indian government's strategy for introducing the claims in the United States was based largely on an assumption that a U.S. jury would likely award a greater amount in damages against the company than would a jury in India.

The following July, Union Carbide presented a preliminary motion to dismiss the case on the grounds that the United States was not the proper location for the filing of the case. Instead, the company argued, Indian courts would be better suited to hear the arguments and make a decision. Union Carbide's lawyers argued that the victims were in India, as was the site of the accident, so a more convenient location for the trial for all parties would be India. Furthermore, they argued, the Indian court system was an adequate venue, with judges who had been properly trained and who had ample experience to be able to handle a case such as this.

On May 12, 1986, U.S. District Court Judge John Keenan agreed with Union Carbide and dismissed the case. As he noted in his opinion:

> The Court thus finds itself faced with a paradox. In the Court's view, to retain the litigation in this forum, as plaintiffs request, would be yet another example of imperialism, another situation in which an established sovereign inflicted its rules, its standards and values on a developing nation. This Court declines to play such a role. The Union of India is a world power in 1986, and its courts have the proven capability to mete out fair and equal justice. To deprive the Indian judiciary of this opportunity to stand tall before the world and to pass judgment on behalf of its own people would be to revive a history of subservience and subjugation from which India had emerged. India and its people can and must vindicate their claims before the independent and legitimate judiciary created there since the Independence of 1947. (In *Union Carbide Corp. Gas Plant Disaster at Bhopal, India*, in December 1984)

In September 1986, the Indian government filed suit for damages worth over $3 billion in the Bhopal District Court. A year and a half later, on February 14, 1989, Union Carbide and the Indian government settled for $470 million—the largest settlement for an industrial accident ever. It dismissed all criminal charges and civil suits in India against Union Carbide and its chairperson. The court ordered the award to be paid in a lump sum by March 31, 1989.

AFTERMATH IN UNITED STATES

Eight months after the leak in Bhopal, on August 11, 1985, 3,800 pounds of chemicals leaked from the Union Carbide facility in Institute, West Virginia. Thousands of nearby residents were exposed to a chemical gas cloud that hovered near the plant, leading to the hospitalization of over 100 residents. Officials later warned that food grown near the Institute plant might be contaminated and should not be eaten. The Occupational Health and Safety Administration (OSHA) cited Union Carbide for willful neglect and fined the company $1.4 million for 221 violations of 55 federal health and safety laws.

Chemical leaks and accidents continued to occur in other localities at other companies. On October 21, 1985, a storage tank with dilute hydrogen sulfide gas leaked in Bayway, New Jersey. In early January 1986, an explosion at a plant in Oklahoma threw hydrofluoric acid into the air, sending over one hundred people to a nearby hospital.

In early 1986, the Environmental Protection Agency released the results from a study of chemical accidents over the previous five years. It listed nearly 7,000 incidents that occurred either at plants or during the transportation of chemicals. These incidents led to the release of roughly 420 million pounds of toxic chemicals; over 130 people had died, more than 1,400 people were injured, and more than 217,000 people had been evacuated (Osterlund 1986).

In response to these domestic accidents, Congress passed the Emergency Planning and Community Right to Know Act of 1986 (EPCRA). This legislation had two purposes. The first was to require each state to provide emergency planning in the event of a toxic chemical leak from an industrial site within its borders. The second was to institute a mandatory reporting requirement for companies to indicate what chemicals were being held at their plants and the safety measures in place to ensure that such chemicals are not released into the surrounding environments.

While EPCRA has set in place a legislative mandate to ensure safety measures for industrial accidents, it has more importantly provided a foundation for liability regarding toxic chemical releases.

CONCLUSION

With the building of newer facilities for the development of chemicals and chemical-based products, the risk of industrial accidents, as we learned through a series of such incidents in the 1970s and 1980s, became greater. The accident at Bhopal has forced the development of new systems and processes, and strategies for minimizing liabilities in an era of increasing development of chemical systems and processes. Bhopal, as we learned, was not a unique phenomenon. While the scale of the accident was greater than that in other places, the occurrence of industrial chemical accidents was common.

Part of the challenge of Bhopal stems from its cross-national level. It raises complex issues around legally resolving conflicts over who may share liability for accidents that involve actors from different countries.

Our modern realities have presented us with the expectation of being able to have available perceived necessities and conveniences for which dangerous compounds are critical ingredients. The products that are produced from these toxic components are so intertwined in our lives that realistically we can't do without the vast majority of them. Imagine a world, for example, without plastics, metals, fertilizers, or any of the hundreds of other items that we view as critical to our day-to-day existence. With their production come by-products that in many cases are harmful to us and to the environment. How we balance production of the items we need and the realities of harmful by-products is one of the central questions in an era of crisis potential and late-modern risks.

14
Oil

When Edwin Drake drilled the first successful oil well near Titusville, Pennsylvania, in the late 1850s, there were few uses for the crude that he was able to extract from the ground. The over eight hundred gallons of oil per day that were produced from his well would be used for lighting, heat, and machine lubrication. The substance that originated from the well was still a century away from the era of oil crises in the late twentieth and early twenty-first centuries.

That Drake drilled only three wells in his lifetime suggests that he didn't predict that the petroleum industry would grow to be such a critical part of the global economy. Yet, within only a few decades, oil had become central to most of our economic systems. From transportation needs to the manufacture of multiple petroleum-based goods, oil was a product that we depended on one in form or another every day. We had also recognized that we had a limited supply of this important source of energy. Such limitations led to continuing expansion of the search for additional sources to supply an ever-growing demand.

By the early twenty-first century, our demand for oil had driven the search to remote locations, with a focus on advancing our technological abilities to extract the oil from such places. This search we rapidly learned, would frequently come with increasing amounts of risk and, once the oil was discovered, the need to transport it across greater distances.

In the spring and summer of 2010, these risks were all too evident with the explosion of the Deepwater Horizon offshore oil platform and the subsequent release of millions of gallons of oil into the Gulf of Mexico. The Deepwater Horizon had been drilling oil at the Macondo well, five thousand feet below the surface of the ocean, which could be reached only with a complex system of technologies and procedures, that made resolving the crisis of a spill that much more difficult.

The Deepwater Horizon oil spill, now recognized as the worst in U.S. history, was one of a series of oil spills over several decades. Each spill, with its resultant environmental damage, has demonstrated a common story—human error, coupled with technological failure, leads to tremendous environmental harm. Policy makers have had to react to these incidents with new approaches to help guard against future failures.

Ironically, in their own unique way, a number of policy decisions have led to these oil crises. Government permits have allowed drilling at previously unimagined depths and in increasingly difficult situations. The government has also encouraged activities that led to companies' taking greater risks in the extraction and processing of oil.

I begin this chapter with an examination of governmental actions that have facilitated the growth in offshore oil drilling. I continue with an examination of several challenges that have arisen in recent decades as a result of the increasing complexity of exploration and extraction. As illustrations, I then examine three spills that have directly or indirectly resulted from remote drilling. The first of these, the 1969 Santa Barbara oil spill, is frequently viewed as one of the first major crises that the U.S. oil industry has faced. I then examine the 1989 case of the *Exxon Valdez*, which until 2010 stood as the worst oil spill in U.S. history. Coupled with several other spills that occurred around the same time, the *Valdez* incident helped to facilitate the passage of the 1990 Oil Pollution Act. I then examine the 2010 Deepwater Horizon crisis, which briefly raised the public consciousness about the risks of deepwater oil extraction. I close the chapter by visiting a series of questions on the risks and challenges of oil development.

HISTORICAL FRAMEWORK

Within several decades of Edwin Drake's drilling for oil in the 1850s, companies were beginning to realize that it would be possible to drill in coastal waters as well as on land. By the early 1900s, a number of coastal communities had drilling piers stretching from beaches into the waters just off the shoreline. These initial piers served as harbingers of what would occur over the next century as the possibility of offshore drilling, and offshore oil pollution, increasingly became a reality.

Congress passed the Oil Pollution Act of 1924 as the first piece of comprehensive legislation addressing the potential danger of oil pollution in nearby coastal waters and out to sea. This act prohibited the release of fuel oil within a radius of three miles offshore. The act was primarily focused on the danger of ships releasing oil and other pollutants in frequently navigated waters, a common occurrence in many of the shared shipping lanes at the time. It did not address accidental spills resulting from the new process of offshore drilling that was taking place in a handful of coastal areas.

By the middle of the twentieth century, interest in the resources under the sea, coupled with advancing technologies to gain access to such resources at increasingly greater depths, led the federal government to identify strategies for extending its accessibility, and that of various commercial entities, farther into the ocean. In September 1945, President Harry Truman declared that the U.S. government regarded the resources of the subsoil and seabed of the continental shelf contiguous to the U.S. coasts to be subject to national jurisdiction. This proclamation was codified in 1953 when Congress enacted the Outer Continental Shelf Land Act, which gave the Department of Interior the responsibility of managing offshore drilling and offshore leases for oil exploration. Within the next decade and a half, the federal government would provide over one thousand leases to companies wanting to drill for oil under the continental seabed.

OIL SPILLS

In March 1967, an oil tanker named the SS *Torrey Canyon* rammed into a reef in the English Channel, sending slightly over nine hundred thousand gallons of Kuwaiti crude oil into international waters off the English shore. The *Torrey Canyon* disaster raised a number of pressing questions about the international maritime law regarding responsibility for oil spills—who should be held liable and under what jurisdiction. The *Torrey Canyon* was American-owned and chartered, registered in Liberia, manned by an Italian captain and crew, contracted by a Dutch company, grounded on a reef in international waters, and destroyed by British military bombers after it rammed into the reef and began leaking oil. It clearly illustrated a number of legal questions around the complexities of oil spills, as well as raised questions regarding possible steps that companies might take to avert future oil spills of this magnitude.

Two years after the *Torrey Canyon* spill, in late January 1969, the seabed near a platform operated by Union Oil six miles off the coast of Santa Barbara began leaking thousands of gallons of crude oil into the ocean. Union Oil had been awarded several federal leases to drill for oil in territorial waters off of the coast of California. The Union Oil well, known as Well A21, was located more than 3,000 feet below the ocean floor, which was another 180 feet below sea level. The well was also near a number of undersea fault lines that ran in several different directions.

The accident had two stages. The first, on January 28, 1969, was an undersea blowout of the three-thousand-foot well. The second occurred when a fault line across the ocean floor broke open and released roughly 80,000–100,000 gallons of oil. The oil created a slick that stretched over 800 square miles. For eleven days, oil oozed across the Santa Barbara Channel at a rate of 1,000 gallons an hour, killing scores of wildlife and blackening thirty miles of California beaches.

After the rupture was closed and the cleanup took place, analysts pointed to several factors that caused the spill. First, it was found that the eruption of one of the platforms was due to inadequate protective casing. It was also found that the U.S. Geological Survey gave the oil company permission to operate the platform according to standards slightly below the traditional ones established by the federal government and the state of California. One of the reasons the company could avoid California's regulations was the placement of the oil rig just slightly beyond the three-mile limit from the California coastline.

Scores of photos showing the oil covering the beaches and the effects on wildlife and marine animals, coupled with numerous citizen advocacy campaigns, helped the nation understand the environmental toll of such a spill. The question that was being asked was, what is the government's role in the prevention and repair of these spills?

As the cleanup efforts from the Santa Barbara spill began, President Nixon noted:

> It is sad that it was necessary that Santa Barbara should be the example that had to bring it to the attention of the American people. What is involved is the use of our resources of the sea and of the land in a more effective way and with more concern for preserving the beauty and the natural resources that are so important to any kind of society that we want for the future. The Santa Barbara incident has frankly touched the conscience of the American people. (Nixon 1969)

The Santa Barbara spill came early in the Nixon presidency and was one of the early indicators of legislative and executive willingness to respond to some environmental concerns of the day. Nixon's observation, coinciding with public support for the development of various environmental regulations, would help to galvanize support for the establishment of the Environmental Protection Agency (EPA) and several other broad approaches to protecting the environment. The central piece of legislation that created the EPA was the National Environmental Policy Act (NEPA), which President Nixon signed into law in 1969.

Three years after NEPA was signed, Congress passed the Water Pollution Control Act Amendments of 1972 also known as the Clean Water Act. This law applied penalties for each barrel of oil or gas spilled as a result of "willful negligence." The act provided a means for managing liabilities for spills, including penalties for such spills. It did not, however, establish effective prevention strategies. The cost of this shortcoming would surface in a matter of a few years.

ALASKA

For a brief period, the Santa Barbara oil spill and the passage of environmental legislation leveraged an ongoing series of activities aimed at conserving energy and protecting the environment. However, the 1973 OPEC oil embargo created a major domestic energy shortage that encouraged policy makers to explore strategies for enhancing access to new sources of energy. One strategy was to identify new areas for energy exploration and development.

Five years before the 1973 oil crisis, more than 10 billion barrels of oil were discovered on the North Slope of Alaska. While this discovery was applauded in anticipation of its ability to address national energy needs, one concern that arose was how to transport the oil from its remote location to areas where it would be of use.

To address this concern, Congress passed the 1973 Alaska Pipeline Act to enable the transport of oil from remote fields identified in Alaska to ports where the oil could be shipped for processing. It was estimated at the time that when the pipeline would be completed in 1977, it would enable the transport of oil across 800 miles of Alaska to the Port of Valdez, located in Alaska's Prince William Sound, where the oil would be loaded onto ships to be transported elsewhere for processing.

VALDEZ AND THE OIL POLLUTION ACT OF 1990

Twelve years after the completion of the Alaskan pipeline, on March 23, 1989, an Exxon ship named after the Valdez port where it was stationed began its journey from Prince William Sound to Southern California. The single-hull supertanker, which was roughly the same size as an aircraft carrier, carried 53 million gallons of oil. At 12:04 Friday morning, the ship ran aground, tearing a hole in its tank and ultimately releasing over 11 million gallons of oil into the sea. Within a few hours, the oil slick surrounding the *Valdez* had spread to an area three miles by five miles around the ship.

As in the case of the Long Beach spill twenty years earlier, the ecological toll quickly become apparent. Prior to the spill, an estimated thirteen thousand sea otters lived in Prince William Sound, as did thousands of sea birds and seemingly countless other forms of marine life. It is estimated that nearly a quarter of the otters in Prince William Sound died as a result of the spill. More than

100,000 seabirds, 247 bald eagles, and 22 orcas were also among the animals reported to have died. It was finally concluded that it would be impossible to know the full extent of the spill on the environment or the animals of Prince William Sound.

Although it received a lot more publicity, the *Valdez* incident was not the only oil spill of 1989. In June, the *World Prodigy* released roughly 290,000 gallons of oil into Narragansett Bay near Rhode Island. That same year, the *Presidente Rivera* spilled 306,000 gallons of oil into the Delaware River. In June 1990, the *Mega Borg*, a supertanker transferring oil to another ship, exploded in the Gulf of Mexico. These accidents led policy makers to the conclusion that the transportation of oil was becoming an increasingly unsafe practice that was in need of some form of governmental oversight. Congress passed the Oil Pollution Act of 1990.

This act sought to build upon what some policy makers viewed as the limitations of the 1972 Clean Water Act's emphasis on post-spill cleanup. The 1990 act, in contrast, focused on preventive measures to minimize the number of oil spills. For example, much of the debate on the 1990 act focused on whether to require double hulls on ships. The *Valdez* had just a single three-quarter-inch plate of steel. Advocates for double hulls argued that with a second hull, either the full amount of *Valdez* oil spilled, or a significant portion, might have been prevented. In the end, advocates for the double hull prevailed.

While components of the 1990 act affected the safety of the oil arena, several important items not mentioned in the act would be critical in later oil crises. First, the act did not refer to oil exploration or transportation in the Gulf of Mexico, which at the time provided a considerable amount of oil for the nation. Outside of Alaska, the Gulf remained the only part of the nation that had shorelines that would remain open to oil exploration.

Second, the 1990 act placed a limit on the liability that a company could face from an oil spill. In deepwater ports, liability would be lowered to a maximum of $350 million, and for accidents occurring farther offshore, the liability limit was established at $75 million. In effect, with such limited liability provisions, the federal government was giving oil companies a safety net for any spills that might occur in the future.

Deepwater Oil Exploration and Government Support

In April 1989, at roughly the same time that the *Valdez* dominated much of the nation's news, Shell Oil announced its discovery of the deepest oil field in the history of oil exploration. Nearly three thousand feet below the surface of the ocean and 140 miles off the coast of Louisiana, the Auger Field presented enormous opportunities for Shell and other companies that would attempt to access its oil deposits.

Getting to this field, however, presented several challenges. First, the seabed at that depth consists of numerous undersea canyons with shifting bottoms prone to earthquakes. The temperature at that depth is near freezing, and the water pressure limits the types of devices that can get to the drill sites. Citing costs associated with such a complex process, Shell argued that to make it economical to explore and extract oil from areas as inaccessible as the Auger Field would require some form of assistance from the federal government.

In November 1995, Congress provided the assistance needed. Spurred by the oil crisis of the 1990s, it passed the Deepwater Royalty Relief Act to facilitate oil exploration in deepwater oilfields such as Auger. The Deepwater Royalty Relief Act waived royalties on deepwater fields leased between 1996 and 2000. The act's impact in terms of encouraging an increase in deepwater exploration leases was almost immediately felt as the number of leases sold in waters half a mile deep or more increased from 50 in 1994 to 1,100 in 1997.

Ten years after the Deepwater Royalty Relief Act, Congress passed the Energy Policy Act of 2005, which provided further incentives for deep water drilling. Oil companies received roughly $2 billion in incentives to seek additional oil and gas in remote pockets of the Gulf. Ultimately, these two pieces of legislation increased opportunities for the extraction of oil from locations that were far more remote than had previously been identified and developed.

Tasked with regulating offshore drilling was the Minerals Management Service (MMS), a federal agency created in 1982 to expand drilling on the outer continental shelf and enhance the domestic energy supply. Part of the challenge that the MMS faced was in ensuring the safety of the deepwater platforms and drilling processes in an extremely complex field of oil exploration. The difficulty was exacerbated by the capacity of the MMS's internal staff. Its engineering staff was a fraction of the size of those at the oil companies it was supposed to monitor, and it had fewer other resources as well. As a result, the agency faced critical questions regarding its ability to monitor the developments of this field of oil exploration and extraction.

Additionally, the MMS confronted potential conflicts stemming from its dual responsibility for both regulating oil exploration and ensuring that the federal government had a continued revenue stream from its leased well sites. With annual royalties of $10 billion from offshore drilling coming into the U.S. Treasury, the MMS was under pressure to balance its regulatory goals with the government's royalty interests.

An example was managing the required testing of the various safety measures. In January 1997, the MMS shifted its requirement that companies test their undersea blowout preventers, a crucial factor in the prevention of explosions on oil rigs, from weekly to biweekly. The change, lobbied for by the oil industry, would save companies around $25 million a year and allow them to expand oil exploration efforts—thus increasing revenues to the companies and the federal government. But this move would be a critical component in a crisis that would occur thirteen years later.

DEEPWATER HORIZON

In 2008, BP, then the fourth largest company in the world, paid $34 million in collaboration with several partner companies to the U.S. government for a ten-year lease to the Mississippi Canyon Block 252, an area that includes several undersea oil deposits in the Gulf of Mexico. BP estimated that oil deposits under the well would vary from 50 million to 1 billion barrels of oil—for an estimated value of up to $86 billion. A central point for accessing these deposits was the Macondo well, located 18,000 feet below the surface of the Gulf.

In February 2009, BP submitted its required exploration plan for the well to the MMS. One of the components of the plan was a projected worst-case scenario for the well if there were to be some form of accident. BP projected that such an incident might blow out almost seven million gallons of oil per day. The company assured the MMS that if this were to occur, it would be able to respond to such a disaster.

To drill at the well site, BP initially leased Transocean's Marianas rig. The Marianas began drilling on October 6, 2009. In early November, the rig sustained significant damages from Hurricane Ida and was sent to shore for repairs. It was later decommissioned.

BP replaced the Marianas with the Deepwater Horizon, a $350 million drilling platform that the company had been leasing since 2001. The Deepwater Horizon was an example of many of the technological advances in drilling for oil far beneath the ocean's surface. In September 2009, it had set the record for drilling the deepest oil and gas well in history at BP's Tiber Field in the Gulf of Mexico. In contrast to older rigs and those in shallower waters that attach to the seafloor with cables or anchors, the Deepwater Horizon was dynamically positioned by a satellite. Ship officers were able to use positioning data provided by the satellite to keep the rig floating on two giant pontoons precisely above the wellhead below.

The Deepwater Horizon arrived at the Macondo well on January 31, 2010. It began drilling on February 15 and was supposed to be finished just three weeks later, on March 8, for a total cost of $96 million.

At 9:49 p.m. on April 20, 2010, several weeks after the Deepwater Horizon was due to have completed its drilling of the Macondo well, a gas bubble raced up 18,360 feet of steel pipe to the drilling rig that sat above. When the bubble reached the rig, it resulted in an explosion and fire that killed eleven workers and injured sixteen others.

The accident began a release of oil into Gulf waters that would continue for the next several months.

AFTER THE ACCIDENT

Less than two weeks after the explosion, the U.S. government proclaimed the spill a national disaster and began to provide resources for the cleanup efforts. For the next several months, crews from BP, the federal government, various state and local agencies, and hundreds of volunteers engaged in an effort to control the well and clean up the affected areas of the Gulf.

Cleaning up the Gulf was a huge challenge, involving not only the Gulf waters but also the various shorelines, beaches, and marshlands that were quickly overrun with oil.

The period following the accident called for an examination its lessons. Several reports, including those from a presidential commission and the U.S. Coast Guard, declared that a number of flaws within the institutional processes regarding oil exploration in the Gulf led to the disaster, including numerous deficiencies within the system itself. As the coast guard noted in its final report, "Although the events leading to the sinking of Deepwater Horizon were set into motion by the failure to prevent a well blowout, the investigation revealed numerous system deficiencies, and acts and omissions by Transocean and its Deepwater Horizon crew, that had an adverse impact on the ability to prevent the magnitude of the disaster" (U.S. Coast Guard 2011, ix).

CONCLUSION

In October 2011, despite the serious criticism directed at the management of the BP Deepwater Horizon crisis in the spring and summer of 2010, the federal government approved a BP plan to drill up to four exploratory oil wells in the Gulf of Mexico. This decision reflected a willingness to tolerate the continued risk of deepwater oil exploration regardless of the experiences from slightly over a year before.

If the number of reports generated on the Deepwater Horizon crisis were to point to any major conclusion that might be drawn, it is that oil exploration at great depths carries with it scores of risks. The willingness to redrill just a short period after the disaster in the Gulf prompts the further conclusion that political interests and significant portions of the public they represent are willing to assume the risk for the sake of obtaining additional oil.

Global energy demands will continue to expand the demand for oil for the foreseeable future, and therefore the desire to identify new sources of energy, particularly oil. The challenge for those working and regulating the industry will be to ensure that they have effective strategies in place to address the risks and to prevent the disasters that could easily result.

Conclusion
Toward New Institutional Frameworks
for Mitigating Risks and Potential Crises

"Haitians, the pain is too heavy for words to express. Let's dry our eyes to rebuild Haiti," enjoined Haitian president Rene Preval in his first broadcast to his nation following the January 12, 2010, earthquake—an event that left more than 200,000 people dead and more than one million people homeless. For Preval and other Haitian leaders who survived the earthquake, the question of what steps to take after a sudden tragedy of this magnitude was likely a question never previously considered, as the scale of the disaster was most certainly never before imaginable.

Over the next several weeks, the media provided hundreds of images from Haiti. We saw the rubble from the earthquake and the bodies of those who did not survive. We watched as tents clustered in soccer stadiums, parks, and other open spaces to provide shelter for thousands of people with no other place to call home. We saw scenes from hospitals where a handful of medical personnel were reduced to removing limbs with the most basic instruments, lest wound infections spread to the rest of patients' bodies. And we heard people express fears about the rainy season to come, bringing with it a cauldron of infectious diseases often expected in the blend of inadequate sanitation, overcrowded settlements, and floodwaters.

Over time, the stories in the media grew quieter. Eventually, they all but disappeared. However, the instability, desperation, and squalor in many of the areas where people settled immediately after the earthquake did not disappear.

In the wake of the earthquake, numerous questions were asked, quickly moving from simply focusing on the extent of the damage to some of the underlying causes. In Haiti, people came to recognize that the crisis wasn't merely the disaster of an earthquake. It was a situation largely rooted in issues of poverty, inadequate governance, and other societal challenges that had been festering in the nation for at least two centuries.

While it has long been designated the poorest country in the Western Hemisphere, Haiti was once considered one of the jewels of the French Empire. Stories of its geographical beauty were spread throughout Europe, which imported most of the coffee and a large percentage of the sugar it consumed from that side of the island known as Hispaniola. By the late eighteenth century, Haiti had become the wealthiest of the French colonies in the Caribbean and was called the "Jewel of the Antilles."

Much of Haiti's wealth derived from the labor provided by its nearly half a million slaves who worked on the various sugar plantations, in the coffee fields, and in the sugar refineries. They outnumbered the French colonizers by a ratio of ten to one, and to maintain a sense of order among its slave population, France instituted one of the more brutal systems of slavery in the Americas.

A turning point came for the nation in 1791 when a group of slaves launched what was the only successful slave revolt in any of the European colonies. By 1804 the nation was free—and its period of economic isolation began. Afraid of the symbol that a nation of slaves who were able to successfully rebel would provide to slaves in the United States, President Thomas Jefferson refused to recognize Haiti as a free nation-state. In 1838, in exchange for its formally recognizing Haiti as a nation and with the backing of the United States, France demanded compensation from the Haitians for what it claimed to be its loss of property, including the slaves, as a result of the successful revolt. Without the support of stronger nations, the Haitian government complied, making its final payment to France in 1883 after having to strip the island of its natural resources to do so. To the north, the United States had decided to formally recognize Haiti in 1864, when the notion of slaves rebelling against their owners was a concept that benefited the Union's campaign against the Confederacy in the War Between the States.

Recognition of Haiti by the United States would bring with it a series of military interventions through the years. The two most significant were a full military operation from 1915 to 1934 in a period of political unrest, when the United States claimed that Haitians were not fit to rule themselves, and a later intervention in 1994 to restore a democratically elected president to power. In between, the nation would be ruled by brutal dictators, some of whom were backed financially and militarily by the United States and who would retain for themselves significant portions of what limited wealth the nation had. Aside from challenges of poor governance and occupation by foreign forces, Haiti would struggle with crises that included persistent poverty, land degradation, and the frequent wrath of hurricanes.

Thus, the Haitian earthquake of January 2010 struck a nation that suffered from generations of poverty and instability—largely the result of forces outside of the nation. Its poverty and politics had long crippled much of the nation and certainly placed it in a difficult position to respond to the disaster that fell upon it.

APPROACH TO THINKING ABOUT DISASTERS AND CRISES

Haiti provides an example of one of the central themes explored throughout this book: the impossibility of disentangling history from the realities of a disaster. It also helps to explore some of the complexities of crises and disasters that are the focus of this book. My central concern in writing *Crisis, Disaster, and Risk* is for current and future policy makers to consider the multiple layers of any disaster and not to merely focus on the short-term factors that might draw only the fastest response.

Disasters and crises have the ability to jolt our thought processes, which, in the short term, might lead us to question societal assumptions that underlie a disaster and how we might respond. For some time following the Lisbon disaster in 1755, the earthquake and tsunami provided justification for questioning the standards of religious belief in Lisbon. For some, it gave cause to further embrace the beliefs they had acquired through the churches in Lisbon. Others, however, saw it as an opportunity to interrogate some of the approaches to faith that had become commonplace. Such examinations sometimes assumed a critical stance on the way practices were interpreted and followed—for example, John Wesley's argument that Lisbon's earthquake was a sign of God's anger at the conduct of the Lisbon people in faith and their daily conduct. Or, take Voltaire's using the quake to challenge the notion of optimism that was being articulated by scores of thinkers at the time.

In the long term, disasters and crises provide an opportunity for us to adjust critical processes in societies in order to adapt and better prepare for the next series of such events. The crisis of HIV/AIDS helped to awaken the world from a sense of complacency we drifted into, believing that we had the scientific and medical knowledge to always confront infectious diseases successfully as they arose. Clearly, as we learned with HIV/AIDS, this was not the case. We struggled to find the cause of the disease. We continue to struggle to find ways to defeat the virus that we now know causes it. We waited as health systems, slow to respond to HIV/AIDS, tried to adapt to assist its victims. In the time that it took to determine the best ways to respond to and research this public health crisis, many more people became infected and many more people died.

HIV/AIDS taught us, however, the need to develop and implement effective public health monitoring and response systems. As a result, when new public health threats such as SARS emerged, we had better mechanisms in place to respond than we had twenty years earlier. Our inability to respond effectively in one health crisis helped us recognize systemic limitations and so to better respond in subsequent health crises.

Our experience with crises and disasters provides us with several areas on which to reflect for building better frameworks for responding to these events. I propose four critical starting points for such reflection: enhancing institutional reflexivity; building an appreciation of risk; understanding disasters and crises as part of our reality; and identifying means to continuously invest in infrastructure.

ENHANCING INSTITUTIONAL REFLEXIVITY

One challenge institutions have is recognizing that they rarely reflect on what they might have learned from either their direct experience or those of other institutions. Each crisis presented in this book provides an opportunity to consider some of the underlying dynamics of a particular crisis or disaster. We can review how organizations respond in both the short and long term in the immediate aftermath and the recovery process that follows a disaster. We can view how organizations use crisis to set in place an effective infrastructure to prepare for the next crisis. We can explore how disasters change thought processes within the institutions affected as well as within the broader societies of which the institutions are a part.

Several of the institutions encountered in this book wrestled with the reality of conflicting missions. The Atomic Energy Commission, for example, had the job of regulating the nuclear energy field and encouraging the development of the nuclear system. The Mineral Management Service also had a dual purpose—to promote the mining of deepwater ocean resources and to regulate such mining activity. Being unable to critically reflect on the difficulty of regulating the same activity they are expected to promote created serious conflicts in influential institutions and in the long run may have limited their effectiveness.

BUILDING AN APPRECIATION OF RISK

Institutions and their actors also need to develop a concept of risk and what it means in their agencies. Central to an appreciation of risk is the recognition that with each of our societal advances we bring a potential societal harm. Whether we identify that harm, and whether we choose to mitigate it, are important considerations as we develop policies for a broad public. Nuclear energy, for example, provides an enormous benefit for communities; it does not produce carbon emissions, and it is relatively inexpensive to produce. Indeed, in an ideal setting, tapping into the potential of nuclear energy would provide us with the ability to, as Lewis Strauss believed, produce energy that is "too cheap to meter." Over the years, government has proved supportive of such development, largely through such legislation as the Price-Anderson Act, which limits companies' liability in case of accidents.

However, as we learned on several occasions, there are serious risks to nuclear energy production. Several reports, including WASH 740, the University of Michigan's report on the Fermi Reactor, and the Rasmussen report, all pointed to the relative safety of nuclear energy. Yet in each case, several years following the release of these reports, incidents at the Fermi reactor, Three Mile Island, Chernobyl, and Fukushima taught us that these reports may have been too optimistic. Accidents could, and did, occur at civilian nuclear power plants.

The dangers from two of these incidents, Chernobyl and Fukushima, stretched across national boundaries and were detected in nations throughout the Northern Hemisphere. In the case of Fermi and Three Mile Island, had the incidents not been contained when they were, similar threats might have spread across a wide geographic area as well.

Risk in this late-modern society is difficult to isolate. Health crises due to known or unknown infectious diseases are one plane ride away from moving from one geographic setting to another. The radiation leak from a nuclear accident can cross national boundaries with just a few wind gusts. The economic toll from a hurricane is felt in markets around the world. Therefore, as we build new systems and approaches for managing the various opportunities presented through newest advances, we need to factor in the means for calculating their risk.

The risks of late modernity and technology are truly of our own making, and preventing them will require a large shift in thought. Underscoring the challenge presented by these risks are notions of technological determinism, or an overconfidence in technology's abilities in ensuring progress, that serve as the foundation of many of our advancements over the past few centuries.

UNDERSTANDING DISASTERS AND CRISES AS PART OF OUR REALITY

Thousands of earthquakes occur in the world every year. Luckily, the number that are felt and, more importantly, the number that cause significant damage are minimal. There are also hundreds of hurricanes and other extreme weather events. Viruses and bacteria, some a slight DNA mutation away from causing widespread illness, surround us. Our reality, simply put, is one in which we will probably face new and continuously emerging crises.

If we think about disasters as constants in our lives, we will be better prepared for them than if we think about them on an occasional basis or only when they occur. This realization does not mean placing ourselves in a continual state of paranoia about the next large hurricane, earthquake, or infectious disease that we will confront. Instead it means that we need to build into our planning processes the means for conceptualizing both the imaginable and the still unimaginable crisis. Imagining some of these scenarios will enable us to consider some of the various challenges that might arise as we confront real crises that we may have once considered only possibilities.

The Hurricane Pam scenario was one conceptualization that a disaster such as Katrina might occur. Coupling it with reports from the local newspaper, the *Times Picayune*, about the lack of preparation for a hurricane of enormous strength and a general history of hurricanes in the region might have enabled officials to be better prepared for Katrina. Such exercises, however, do entail being willing to put in place some plans for handling these possible disasters.

IDENTIFYING MEANS TO CONTINUOUSLY INVEST IN INFRASTRUCTURE

Continued infrastructure investment to identify and prepare for possible crises is a central strategy that will help manage the risks and perhaps the realities that we will encounter in the future. Two categories of infrastructure should be considered. The first is physical. As long as people live in New Orleans, a system of levees is an important infrastructure to maintain. Such an investment, however, must be considered alongside the reality that levees and other structures meant to minimize risks may also create further risks. A levee system may assist in keeping a city dry, but if not repaired or occasionally strengthened, levees can break. They also have the power to move waterways outside the direction of their natural flow, adding more potential risk as lands that are based on river silt—as is the case in much of southern Louisiana—are moved from their natural settling places.

The second critical infrastructure is the capability of institutions involved in crisis relief and emergency response to monitor and learn. Investments in the Global Health Intelligence Network and the Global Outbreak Alert and Response Network enabled the world health community to learn about and respond to SARS much faster than it would have otherwise, thus containing what could have become a much larger crisis. Evaluation of the response to the 2004 tsunami in Indonesia assisted the relief-and-recovery community to better respond to the Haiti crisis than it might otherwise have done.

Government also has played a role in attempting to minimize the various risks once they have been identified. Institutions such as the Atomic Energy Commission and later the Nuclear Regulatory Agency have evolved to develop strategies for handling nuclear risks. Treaties and their monitoring institutions have played numerous roles in ensuring that efforts do have some safety considerations. Legislation passed in response to such incidents as the *Exxon Valdez* spill, the gas leaks at Bhopal and Incident, and toxic waste seepage at Love Canal is evidence of government assuming a more active role in helping to address the risks it has had some role in creating. As we expand our horizons for development in this late-modern era, we will need to identify ways to expand the range of options for controlling the potential challenges that might result.

CONSIDERATIONS AND CONCLUSIONS

Since late-modern realities will continue to bring numerous potential risks for humankind, policy makers and those influencing political and administrative processes will need to continue to develop means for taking into account, and preparing for, the crises that we will encounter in the foreseeable future.

Governments need to explore how to balance the risks and rewards that come with the implementation of various policies.

How might we facilitate the training of policy makers who are comfortable with some of the reflexive modes of thinking that allow for adequate balancing of such perspectives? Are there proper or effective training or educational strategies that can develop institutions and technological knowledge among people who frame strategies for preparing for and responding to various crises? Those who draft legislation that encourages risk should be prepared to take into account as well a list of methods to allay those risks.

History has certainly taught us, through floods, tsunamis, viral outbreaks, and nuclear crises that disasters are very much a part of the human experience. However, history has also taught us that we can—through long-term individual and institutional determination—identify strategies for minimizing the impact of such disasters in the future.

Bibliography

Abraham, Thomas. 2007. *Twenty-First Century Plague: The Story of SARS*. Baltimore: Johns Hopkins University Press.

Acheson, Dean. 1987. *Present at the Creation: My Years in the State Department*. New York: W.W. Norton.

"AIDS: Risks and Responsibilities." 1985. Editorial, *Washington Post*, August 14, A22.

Allison, Graham. 2005. *Nuclear Terrorism: The Ultimate Preventable Catastrophe*. New York: Macmillan.

Altman, Lawrence K. 1982. New homosexual disorder worries health officials. *New York Times*, May 11.

American Meteorological Society. 1986. Is the United States headed for hurricane disaster? A statement of concern. *Bulletin of the American Meteorological Society* 67(5): 537–538.

Annan, Kofi. 2004. Secretary-General Kofi Annan and UN's Emergency Relief Coordinator Jan Egeland at press conference on Asian tsunami disaster. December 30. www.un.org/apps/sg/offthecuff.asp?nid=660 (accessed May 18, 2012).

Atwater, B.F., Marco Cisternas V. Joanne Bourgeois, Walter C. Dudley, James W. Hendley II, and Peter H. Stauffer. 1999. Surviving a tsunami—Lessons from Chile, Hawaii, and Japan. Circular 1187. Reston, VA: U.S. Dept. of the Interior, U.S. Geological Survey.

Beck, Ulrich. 1992. *Risk Society: Towards a New Modernity*. Thousand Oaks: Sage Publications.

———. 1994. The Reinvention of Politics: Towards a Theory of Reflexive Modernization in Ulrich Beck, Anthony Giddens, and Scott Lash. *Reflexive Modernization: Politics, Tradition, and Aesthetics in the Modern Social Order*. Cambridge: Polity Press.

Braddock. 1755; repr. 1789. Letter from Mr. Braddock to Dr. Sandby, Chancellor of the Diocese of Norwich, November 13. *European Magazine and London Review* (London: Philological Society of London) 16(July): 424–432.

Braine, T. 2006. Was 2005 the year of natural disasters? *Bulletin of the World Health Organization* 84(1): 4–6.

Branner, J.C. 1913. Earthquakes and structural engineering. *Bulletin of the Seismological Society of America*, March.

Brearley, Harry Chase. 1916. *The History of the National Board of Fire Underwriters: Fifty Years of a Civilizing Force*. New York: Frederick A. Stokes Co.

Byerly, Carol. 2005. *The Fever of War*. New York: New York University Press.

Carrigan, William C. 1905. *The History and Antiquities of the Diocese of Ossory*. Dublin: Sealy, Bryers, and Walker.

Carson, Rachel. 1962. *Silent Spring*. New York: Houghton Mifflin.

Carter, Jimmy. 1980. Health and medical care for Love Canal area residents. Statement on a request to Congress for appropriations. October 24. Online by Gerhard Peters and John T. Woolley, *The American Presidency Project*. www.presidency.ucsb.edu/ws/?pid=45364 (accessed July 18, 2012).

Centers for Disease Control and Prevention (CDC). 1986. Epidemiological notes and reports: Acquired immunodeficiency syndrome (AIDS) among blacks and Hispanics. *Morbidity and Mortality Weekly Report* 35(42).

———. 2003. CDC Lab Analysis Suggests New Coronavirus May Cause SARS. Press release, March 24. www.cdc.gov/media/pressrel/r030324.htm (accessed November 10, 2011).

———. 2010. The History of Malaria, an Ancient Disease. February 8. www.cdc.gov/malaria/about/history/ (accessed November 29, 2011).

Chase, Marilyn. 2003. *The Barbary Plague: The Black Death in Victorian San Francisco*. New York: Random House.

Christianson, Scott. 2010. *Fatal Airs: The Deadly History and Apocalyptic Future of Lethal Gases That Threaten Our World*. Santa Barbara: ABC-CLIO.

Clarfield, Gerard H., and William Wiecek. 1984. *Nuclear America: Military and Civilian Nuclear Power in the United States, 1940–1980*. New York: Harper & Row.

Clendinen, Dudley. 1983. AIDS spreads pain and fear among young and healthy alike. *New York Times*, June 17.

Cline, Isaac. 1999. *Storms, Floods, and Sunshine*. New Orleans: Pelican Publishing.

Cline, Joseph. 2000. *When the Heavens Frowned*. Gretna: Pelican Publishing.

Crosby, Alfred W. 1976. *Epidemic and Peace, 1918*. Westport: Greenwood Press.

Dean, Gordon. 1952. The Atom in National Defense. Address before the 75th Annual Meeting of the American Bar Association, San Francisco, September 17.

Defoe, Daniel. 1896. *A Journal of the Plague Year*. London: Longmans Green.

Dow, Lorenzo. 1849. *The dealings of God, man and the devil: As exemplified in the life, experience and travels of Lorenzo Dow, in a period of over half a century*. New York: Sheldon, Lamport & Blakeman.

Eisenhower, Dwight D. 1953. Atoms for Peace. Speech delivered to the 470th Plenary Meeting of the United Nations General Assembly, December 8.

Eleventh Judicial Circuit of Florida (Miami). 1976. *Final Report of the Grand Jury in the Circuit Court of the Eleventh Judicial Circuit of Florida in and for the County of Dade*, Fall Term 1975. Filed May 11, 1976.

———. 1990. *A Critique of Construction Regulation*. Final Report of the Grand Jury in the Circuit Court of the Eleventh Judicial Circuit of Florida in and for the County of Dade, Fall Term 1989. Filed May 15, 1990.

Epidemic lessons against next time: Dr. Copeland tells why New York got off easier than other cities. 1918. *New York Times*, November 17.

Faraday, Michael. 1855. Observations on the filth of the Thames. Letter to the Editor of *The Times*. In *Reports from Commissioners: 1854–55*, vol. 7, General Board of Health (Medical Council). Session 12 December 1854–14 August 1855. London: George E. Eyre and William Spottiswoode.

Farmbry, Kyle. 2009. *Administration and the Other: Explorations of Diversity and Marginalization in the Political Administrative State*. New York: Rowman & Littlefield.

Fortun, Kim. 2001. *Advocacy After Bhopal.* Chicago: University of Chicago Press.

Friedman, Meyer, and Gerald W. Freidland. 1998. *Medicine's 10 Greatest Discoveries.* New Haven: Yale University Press.

Freidrich, Otto. 1986. *The End of the World: A History.* New York: Fromm International.

George, Rose. 2008. *The Big Necessity.* London: Portobello Books.

Gibbs, Lois Marie. 1998. *Love Canal: The Story Continues . . .* Stony Creek: New Society.

Giddens, Anthony. 1990. *The Consequences of Modernity.* Stanford: Stanford University Press.

———. 1991. *Modernity and Self-Identity: Self and Society in the Late Modern Age.* Stanford: Stanford University Press.

———. 1994. Living in a Post Traditional Society. In Ulrich Beck, Anthony Giddens, and Scott Lash. *Reflexive Modernization: Politics, Tradition, and Aesthetics in the Modern Social Order.* Cambridge: Polity Press.

Gilbert, Grove Karl. 1909. Earthquake Forecasts: Future Possibilities. *Scientific American Supplement. No. 1732.*

Gomberg, Henry Jacob. 1957. Report on the possible effects on the surrounding population of an assumed release of fission products into the atmosphere from a 300 megawatt nuclear reactor located at Lagoona Beach, Michigan. Ann Arbor: Engineering Research Institute.

Gorbachev, Mikhail. 1996. *Memoirs.* New York: Doubleday.

Gorgas, William Crawford. 1915. *Sanitation in Panama.* New York: D. Appleton.

Green, Casey Edward, and Shelly Henley Kelly (eds.). 2000. *Through a Night of Horrors: Voices from the 1900 Galveston Storm.* College Station: Texas A&M University Press.

Hansen, Gladys, and Emmet Condon. 1989. *Denial of Disaster: The Untold Story and Photographs of the San Francisco Earthquake and Fire of 1906.* San Francisco: Cameron & Co.

Herlihy, David. 1997. *The Black Death and the Transformation of the West.* Cambridge, MA: Harvard University Press.

Hernan, Robert Emmet. 2010. *This Borrowed Earth: Lessons from the Fifteen Worst Environmental Disasters Around the World.* New York: Palgrave Macmillan.

Hewitt, Fred. 1906. Wreck of city's buildings awful. *San Francisco Examiner,* April 20. www.sfmuseum.net/1906/ew4.html (accessed May 18, 2012).

Hoffman, David. 2010. *The Dead Hand: The Untold Story of the Cold War Arms Race and Its Dangerous Legacy.* New York: Random House Digital.

Horrox, Rosemary (ed.). 1994. *The Black Death.* Manchester, England: Manchester University Press.

Hunter, Susan S. 2003. *Black Death: AIDS in Africa.* New York: Palgrave Macmillan.

Jaffe, Ina. 2005. Analysis: Los Angeles studies Katrina cleanup. Morning Edition (National Public Radio), September 9.

Johnson, Lyndon Baines. 1965. The President's remarks upon arrival at New Orleans Municipal Airport. Transcript, September 10. www.lbjlib.utexas.edu/johnson/AV.hom/Hurricane/audio_transcript.shtm (accessed November 27, 2011).

Johnson, Steven. 2006. *The Ghost Map: The Story of London's Most Terrifying Epidemic—and How It Changed Science, Cities, and the Modern World.* New York: Penguin.

Kelly, Cynthia C. (ed.). 2007. *The Manhattan Project.* New York: Black Dog & Leventhal.

Kemeny, John. 1979. *Report of the President's Commission on the Accident at Three Mile Island.* New York: Pergamon.

Kluger, Jeffrey. 2004. *Splendid Solution: Jonas Salk and the Conquest of Polio.* New York: G.P. Putnam's Sons.

Larson, Erik. 1999. *Isaac's Storm.* New York: Crown.

Lay, James S., Jr. 1953. *A Report to the National Security Council by the Executive Secretary on Basic National Security Policy.* NSC 162/2, October 30. Washington, DC. www.fas.org/irp/offdocs/nsc-hst/nsc-162-2.pdf.

A Letter from Camp Devins [sic], Mass. 1918. September 29. PBS, American Experience: Influenza 1918: Primary resources. www.pbs.org/wgbh/americanexperience/features/primary-resources/influenza-letter/ (accessed November 10, 2011).

Liebniz, Gottfried Willhelm [1710 (1951)]. *Theodicy: Essay on the Goodness of God, the Freedom of Man, and the Origin of Evil.* London: Routledge & Kegan Paul Limited.

London, Jack. 1906. "The Story of an Eyewitness." May 5. *Collier's Magazine.* On-line at: www.sfmuseum.org/List5/jlondon.htm/ (accessed July 18, 2012).

Luis Sancho v. U.S. Department of Energy (USDC Hawaii, March 14, 2008).

McQuaid, John, and Mark Schleifstein. 2002. The big one (part 2 of a special report, Washing Away). *Times-Picayune,* June 24.

Mendis, Kamini, Aafje Rietveld, et al. 2009. From malaria control to eradication: The WHO perspective. *Tropical Medicine and International Health* 14(7): 802–809.

Najera, J.A. 1989. Malaria and the work of WHO. *Bulletin of the World Health Organization* 67(3): 229–243.

Newhouse, John. 1989. *War and Peace in the Nuclear Age.* New York: Alfred A. Knopf.

Nitze, Paul H. 1976. Assuring strategic stability in an era of détente. *Foreign Affairs* 54(2): 207–232.

Nixon, Richard. 1969. Remarks following inspection of oil damage at Santa Barbara beach. March 21. Online by Gerhard Peters and John T. Woolley, *The American Presidency Project,* www.presidency.ucsb.edu/ws/?pid=1967.

O'Connor, Charles James, Francis H. McLean, Helen Swett Artieda, James Marvin Motley, Jessica Blanche Peixotto, and Mary Roberts Coolidge. 1913. *San Francisco Relief Survey: The Organization and Methods of Relief Used After the Earthquake and Fire of April 18, 1906.* New York: Survey Associates, publisher for the Russell Sage Foundation.

Oppenheimer, J. Robert. 1953. Atomic weapons and American policy. *Foreign Affairs* 31(4): 525–535.

Oshinsky, David M. 2005. *Polio: An American Story.* New York: Oxford University Press.

Osterlund, Peter. 1986. Is the U.S. chemical industry safe? *Christian Science Monitor,* January 27.

Perlman, David. 2006. The great quake: 1906–2006/Bracing for the next 'big one.' *San Francisco Chronicle,* April 18.

Perrow, Charles. 1984. *Normal Accidents: Living with High Risk Technologies.* New York: Basic Books.

Pope, Alexander. 1734 (1867). *An Essay on Man.* New York: Samuel R. Wells, Publisher.

Priest, Andrew. 2006. *Kennedy, Johnson, and NATO: Britain, America and the Dynamics of Alliance.* New York: Taylor & Francis.

Prince, Samuel Henry. 1920. *Catastrophe and Social Change: Based on Sociological Study of The Halifax Disaster.* New York: Columbia University.

Quint, Michael. 1993. A year after Hurricane Andrew, insurers maneuver to lower risk. *New York Times,* December 28.

Rangel, Charles B. 1987. Blacks, Hispanics, and AIDS. *Washington Post,* August 18.

Rasmussen, Norman C. 1974. *Reactor Safety Study: An Assessment of Accident Risks in U.S. Commercial Nuclear Power Plants,* vol. 1. Washington, DC: Nuclear Regulatory Commission.

Reeves, Richard. 1994. *President Kennedy: Profiles in Power.* New York: Simon and Schuster.

Restore America's Estuaries and the National Oceanic and Atmospheric Administration (NOAA). 2002. Cover letter. In *A National Strategy to Restore Coastal and Estuarine Habitat.* Report, April. Washington, DC: NOAA. www.era.noaa.gov/pdfs/entire.pdf (accessed July 18, 2012).

Sachs, Jessica Snyder. 2007. *Good Germs, Bad Germs: Health and Survival in a Bacterial World.* New York: Macmillan.

Schleifstein, Mark, and John McQuaid. 2002. In harm's way (part 1 of a special report, Washing Away). *Times-Picayune,* June 24.

Schwartz, John. 2010. Five years after Katrina, 350 miles of protection. *New York Times,* August 24, A1.

Sedgwick, Charles B. 1906. The fall of San Francisco: Some personal observations. *American Builders' Review,* July. www.sfmuseum.org/1906.2/ew20.html (accessed November 20, 2011).

Sharrar, Robert G., Alfred S. Bogucki, and John Uffelman. n.d. Some aspects of the 1918–19 influenza epidemic in Philadelphia and the United States. *Philadelphia Medicine.*

Shepard, F.P., G.A. Macdonald, and D.C. Cox. 1949. *The Tsunami of April 1, 1946.* Berkeley: University of California Press.

Shilts, Randy. 2007. *And the Band Played On: Politics, People, and the AIDS Epidemic.* New York: Macmillan.

Short, James F. 1984. The social fabric at risk: Toward the social transformation of risk analysis. *American Sociological Review* 49(6): 711–725.

Smith, Brice. 2007. *Insurmountable Risks: The Dangers of Using Nuclear Power to Combat Global Climate Change.* Takoma Park, MD: IEER Press.

Snow, John. 1855. *On the Mode and Communication of Cholera.* London: John Churchill.

Stolberg, Sheryl Gay. 1998. Epidemic of silence: A special report—Eyes shut, Black America ravaged by AIDS. *New York Times,* June 29.

Twain, Mark. 1873. *Roughing It.* New York: American Publishing Company.

Union Carbide Corp. Gas Plant Disaster at Bhopal, India, in December 1984. 634 F. Supp 842, 867 (SDNY 1986).

United Nations Children's Fund (UNICEF). 2006. *Africa's Orphaned Generations.* Report. New York: United Nations Children's Fund.

United States v. Hooker Chemicals & Plastics Corp., 850 F. Supp 993 (1994).

U.S. Atomic Energy Commission. 1957. *Theoretical Possibilities and Consequences of Major Accidents in Large Nuclear Power Plants.* Washington, DC: U.S. Atomic Energy Commission.

U.S. Coast Guard. 2011. *Report of Investigation into the Circumstances Surrounding the Explosion, Fire, Sinking and Loss of Eleven Crew Members Aboard the Mobile Offshore Drilling Unit Deepwater Horizon in the Gulf of Mexico, April 20–22, 2010.* Washington, DC: U.S. Coast Guard.

U.S. Geological Survey (USGS). 2009. Major Quake Likely to Strike San Francisco Bay Region Between 2003 and 2032. Earthquake Hazards Program, January 29. http://earthquake.usgs.gov/research/seismology/wg02/ (accessed November 10, 2011).

Voltaire. 1741. *Letters Concerning the English Nation.* London: Printed for C. Davis.

———. 1901. Candide. In *The Works of Voltaire*, ed. John Morley, William Fleming, and Oliver Herbrand Gordon Leigh. New York: E.R. Dumont.

———. 2000. Preface to the poem on the Lisbon disaster. *Candide and Related Texts*, trans. David Wootton. Indianapolis, IN: Hackett.

Wells, Herbert George. 1914. *The World Set Free: A Story of Mankind.* New York: E.P. Dunnton.

Wesley, John. 1827. *The Works of the Rev. John Wesley*, vol. 8: *A plain account of Christian perfection; The appeals to men of reason and religion; Principles of the Methodists, &c.* New York: J & J Harper.

White, Gilbert and J. Eugene Haas. 1975. *Assessment of Research on Natural Hazards.* Cambridge: MIT Press.

Winchester, Simon. 2006. *A Crack in the Edge of the World.* New York: Harper Collins.

World Health Organization (WHO). 2003. Agenda item 14.16: Revision of the International Health Regulations and WHA Resolution 56.29. 56th World Health Assembly (WHA), Geneva, May 28.

———. 2011. *A Decade of Partnerships and Results.* Progress and Impact Series, no. 7, September. Geneva: World Health Organization.

X (1947) The Sources of Soviet Conduct. *Foreign Affairs.* 25(4): 566–582.

Ziegler, Philip. 1971. *The Black Death.* New York: Harper Perennial.

Index

A

Acheson, Dean, 132
Adams, John, 75
The Advancement of Learning (Bacon), 59
Alaska Pipeline Act (1973), 163
American Meteorological Society, 38–39
And the Band Played On (Shilts), 102
Annan, Kofi, 16, 105
Anti-Ballistic Missile Treaty, 130–131
Antibiotics, 97
Army Corps of Engineers, 41, 43
Army Signal Corps, 32
Atomic bomb development, 122–123
  movement toward use, 123–124
Atomic Energy Act (1946), 134
Atomic Energy Act (1954), 134–135
Atomic Energy Commission, 135, 138, 174, 177
"Atoms for Peace" (Eisenhower speech), 128
Assessment of Research on Natural Hazards, (Haas), xvi

B

Bacon, Francis, 59
Bhopal accident, 119, 151–154, 177
  aftermath in U.S., 156
  case/litigation, 154–155
Bienville, Sieur de, 30, 41
Blue, Rupert, 25, 75–77
Boyle, Robert, 59
BP Deepwater Horizon oil spill, 119, 166–168
Braner, John, 26
Brian, Eliza, 1
Brutland, Gro, 96
Built environment
  building codes, 39–40
  choices in, 31
  infrastructure investment, 176–177
  migration and postwar areas, 35–36

C

Candau, Marcolino Gomes, 90
Candide (Voltaire), 10
Carson, Bob, 124
Carson, Rachel, 94
Carter, Jimmy, 38, 148
Caruso, Enrique, 19
Catastrophe and Social Change, (S.H. Prince), xiii

Centers for Disease Control and Prevention (CDC), 50, 85, 94, 101, 103
CERN Large Hadron Collider, 117
Chadwick, Edwin, 68, 71–72
Chernobyl disaster, 119, 141, 175
Chicago earthquakes, 1–2
Chisholm, Brock, 89–90
Cholera, 65–66
  London's outbreak, 68–70
  Soho outbreak, 70–71
Clean Water Act, 147, 162, 164
Clemens, Samuel, 21
Cline, Isaac, 32–33
Clyne, John, 56
Cold War era
  middle years, 128–131
  nuclear risk, 126–128
  post-era nuclear threats, 131–132
Comprehensive Environmental Response, Compensation, and Liability Act (CERCLA), 149
Compton, Arthur H., 122
Convention on Assistance in the Case of a Nuclear Accident or Radiological Emergency (the Assistance Convention), 142
Convention on Nuclear Safety (CNS), 142
Cox, D. C., 13
Crisis response, 172–173
  Hyogo framework to, 18
  nongovernmental response to, 6
Cuban Missile Crisis (1962), 129
Curie, Pierre and Marie, 120

D
Dalton, John, 120
Dean, Gordon, 135

Deep-ocean Assessment and Reporting of Tsunamis (DART) system, 14, 16
Deepwater Horizon (BP) oil spill, 119, 158–159
Deepwater oil exploration, 165–166
Deepwater Royalty Relief Act, 165
DeFoe, Daniel, 51
Disease surveillance, 90
Drake, Edwin, 158–159
Drinking water safety, 67
Dubos, Rene, 97, 100
Dulles, John Foster, 127

E
Earthquakes
  Haitian earthquake (2010), 170–172
  Lisbon (1755) disaster, 5, 9–10
  progressive-era revival, 19–20
  urban safety and, 21–22
  See also San Francisco earthquake (1906).
Einstein, Albert, 122
Eisenhower, Dwight D., 127–128
Emergency Planning and Community Rights to Know Act of 1986 (EPCRA), 156
Energy Policy Act of 2005, 165
Engebretsen, Ray, 99
Environment awareness, 147
Environmental Protection Agency (EPA), 148, 156, 162
Epidemiology, 49
An Essay on Man (Pope), 7
Europe Enlightenment, 7
European Center for Nuclear Research (CERN), 117
Executive Order 12148, 38

Exxon Valdez oil spill, 119, 159, 163–164, 177

F

Federal Emergency Management Agency (FEMA), 38, 40, 42
Federal Highway Act (1956), 36
Fermi, Enrico, 121
Fermi reactor incident, 137–138, 175
Findlay, Carlos, 92
Fleming, Alexander, 84–85
Flood Control Act, xiv
Fracastoro, Girolamo, 62
Fukushima nuclear accident, 119, 142, 175

G

Galen of Pergamon, 57
Galveston hurricane (1900), 4, 31
   growth of city, 31–32
   post-storm actions, 34–35
   seawall arguments, 32–34
   weather prediction and control, 35
Gay Men's Health Crisis, 102
Germ theory, 48–49, 65
   London's cholera epidemic and, 72
Gibbs, Louise, 147
Gilbert, Grove Karl, 27
Glasnost (openness), 131
Global Fund to Fight HIV/AIDS, Tuberculosis, and Malaria, 106
Global Malaria Control Strategy, 96
Global Program on AIDS (GPA), 103
Global public health, 47–50, 177.
   anticipation of crisis, 108–110
   global health surveillance, 110–112
   historical context of, 47–50
   modern era fears, 115–116

Global public health *(continued)*
   plague, 51–54
   See also HIV/AIDS; Severe acute respiratory syndrome (SARS)
Godwin, Ron, 101–102
Gorbachev, Mikhail, 130–131
Gorgas, William, 91–93
Governmental responses, 16
Gower, John, 58
Grant, Ulysses, 32
"The Great Assize" (Wesley), 12
Groves, Leslie, 123
Gutenberg, Johann, 58

H

Hadron Collider, 117
Hahn, Otto, 121
Haitian earthquake (2010), 170–172
Hazardous waste, 143–144
   environmental awareness, 147
Health infrastructure, 74
Henle, Jakob, 47–48, 72
Herlihy, David, 58
Hiroshima and Nagasaki atomic bombings, 124–128, 133
History of the Peloponnesian War (Procopius), 52
HIV/AIDS, 50, 98–99, 106–107, 173
   in 21st century, 105–106
   in 1990s, second decade, 103–105
   appearance and spread of, 100–101
   as global crisis, 103
   historical overview of crisis, 99–100
   stigmas and responses to, 101–103
Hooker Company, 143, 145–147
Human suffering, 5
Humphrey, Hubert, 94

Hurricane Andrew (1992), 38–40
Hurricane Betsy (1965), 37
Hurricane Camille (1969), 37
Hurricane Carla (1961), 36
Hurricane Donna (1960), 36
Hurricane Katrina (2004), 4, 31,
    40–44
  aftermath of, 42–43
  rebuilding, 43–44
Hurricane Pam scenario, 42, 176
Hurricanes, 4.
  building codes and, 39–40
  limits of built environment, 30
  locality choice and, 30
  PAM scenario, 42, 176
  preparation for, 37–38
  risk in U.S., 38–39
  Saffir-Simpson Damage Potential
    Scale, 38
  See also Galveston hurricane
    (1900).
Hyogo Framework for Action
    (HFA), 18

I
Indian Ocean tsunami (2004), 3, 5
  crisis response to, 16
Industrial accidents, 119, 151–152
  Bhopal accident, 151–154
  chemical leaks, 156
Infectious diseases, 47–48, 65.
  disease surveillance, 90
  eradication of, 85
  malaria, 91–95
  polio, 86–88
  public health infrastructures and,
    73–75, 111
  smallpox, 88–91
  See also Plague.

Influenza pandemic (1918), 49,
    73–74
  background of war, 75–76
  in New York City and
    Philadelphia, 79–82
  urban spread, 76–82
Infrastructure investment, 176–177
Institutional reflexivity, 174
International Atomic Energy
    Agency (IAEA), 127, 131
International Atomic Energy
    Association (IAEA), 141–142

J
Jenner, Edward, 89
Johnson, Lyndon B., 37, 90
Joint United Nations Program on
    HIV/AIDS (UNAIDS), 104
Jones, Robert T., 31
A Journal of the Plague Year (Defoe),
    51
Justinian Plague, 52

Keen, William, 86
Keenan, John, 155
Kennan, George, 126
Kennedy, John F., 94, 129
King Charles II, 59
King John V, 11
King Jose I, 11
Kistiakowsky, George B., 129
Kobe Japan earthquake (1995), 17

L
Langmuir, Alexander, 90
Law, Charles, 34
Lederberg, Joseph, 97, 100
Leeuwenhoek, Anton, 47–48
Leibniz, Gottfried, 7, 9

Letters Concerning the English Nation (Voltaire), 7
Lewis, Robert A., 124
Limited Test Ban Treaty, 129
Lisbon (1755) disaster, 3, 5–6, 8, 172–173
  as challenge to optimism, 9
  earthquake and tsunami, 8–11
  as God's retribution, 12–13
  health considerations, 11–12
  rebuilding plan, 11
  relief efforts, 12–13
  role of government in, 11–12
Loma Prieta earthquake (1989), 28
London, Jack, 23
Long Beach oil spill, 119
Love Canal, 119, 143–144, 177
  crisis emerges, 147–149
  historical background to, 144–146
  post-crisis changes, 149–150
Love, William, 144–146

M
MacDonald, G. A., 13
McNamara, Robert, 129
McQuaid, John, 40–42
Malaria, 91–95
  Global Malaria Control Strategy, 96
  Roll Back Malaria effort, 96
  vector-based approach to, 91–94
Manhattan Project, 121, 123
March of Dimes, 87–88
Marshall, George C., 96
Meade, Richard, 62
Medical optimism, 85
Melo, Sebastian Jose de Carvalho (Pombal), 11
Miasms and Contagia (Henle), 47

Minerals Management Service (MMS), 166, 174
Montesquieu, 60
Mutual assistance, 6
Mutually Assured Destruction, 129

N
Namatar, 52
National Board of Fire Underwriters, 22
National Environmental Policy Act (NEPA), 147, 162
National Hurricane Center, 37–38
National Oceanic and Atmospheric Association (NOAA), 44
Natural disasters
  as crisis, 1–4
  earthquakes, 1–2
  human choice in, 3
  hurricanes, 4
  tsunamis, 3
New Atlantis (Bacon), 59
New Madrid Sequence, 1–2
New Orleans
  "filling the bowl" scenario (McQuaid and Schleifstein), 40–41
  geographical changes in, 41
  Great Hurricane (1722), 30
  Hurricane Betsy (1965), 37
New York State Department of Health (DOH), 148
Newlands, A. R., 120
Newton, Isaac, 60
Nitze, Paul, 130
Nixon, Richard M., 147, 162
Nongovernmental institutions, 6
Novum Organum (Bacon), 59

Nuclear energy
  1970s safety issues, 138–139
  changes of accidents, 136–137
  Chernobyl accident, 141
  civilian issues, 141–142
  civilian use of, 134
  Fermi reactor incident, 137–138
  optimism and risks of, 133–134,
    175
  potential acknowledged, 134–137
  risks realized, 137–138
  safety issues of, 134
  Three Mile Island accident,
    139–140
Nuclear era
  Cold War era and, 126–132
  development of atomic bomb,
    122–123
  Hiroshima and Nagasaki, 124–128
  history and scientific
    advancement in, 121–122
  Manhattan Project, 122–123
  multiple crises of, 120–121
  Mutually Assured Destruction,
    129
  NSC 162/2, 127
  post-cold war threats, 131–132
Nuclear Nonproliferation Treaty,
  130
Nuclear Regulatory Commission
  (NRC), 138, 177
Nuclear risk, 118–119
  Cold War era, 126–132
Nuclear weapons, 120

O
Occupational Health and Safety
  Administration (OSHA), 156
Oil exploration, 119

Oil pollution, 158
Oil Pollution Act (1924), 160
Oil Pollution Act (1990), 159,
  163–164
Oil spills, 160–162
  in Alaska, 162–163
  Exxon Valdez, 163–164
  liability and jurisdiction of, 161
On Contagion and Contagious Disease and
  Their Cure (Fracastoro), 62
Oppenheimer, J. Robert, 122–123,
  126–127
Optimism
  European Enlightenment and, 7
  reflections on, 5
Outer Continental Shelf Land Act,
  160

P
Pacific Tsunami Warning Center,
  13–14
Pasteur, Louis, 47–48, 72
Pasteurization, 47
Penicillin, 84–85
Perestroika (restructuring), 131
Pesticides, 95
Pizarro, Francisco, 89
Plague
  in 1300s, effects of crisis, 54–58
  in 1600s, emergence of science,
    59–61
  in 1700s, 61–63
  ancient world accounts of, 51–52
  Europe's plague years, 53
  Marseilles (1720 and 1721), 51
Polio, 86–88
  infrastructure to combat, 87–88
Pope, Alexander, 7, 9
Potsdam Proclamation, 124

Present at the Creation (Acheson), 132
Price-Anderson Act (1957), 134, 136, 175
The Principia (Newton), 60
Procopius, 52
Public health. *See* Global public health
Public health infrastructure, 74–75

Q
Quarantines, 62–63, 108

R
Rangel, Charles, 103
Rasmussen, Norman, 138, 175
Reagan administration, 130–131
Reed, Walter, 92
Report on the Sanitary Conditions of the Labouring Population of Great Britain (Chadwick), 68
Rina, Patra, 14–15
Risk concept, 174–175
Roosevelt, Franklin D., 86–87, 122
Roosevelt, Theodore, 92
Ross, Ronald, 91
Roughing It (Clemens), 21
Royal Society, 59–60
  Philosophical Transaction, 47
Rubin, Benjamin, 90
Rusk, Dean, 129

S
Saffir, Herbert, 37–38
Saffir-Simpson Damage Potential Scale, 38
Salk, Jonas, 87

San Francisco earthquake (1906), 19–23
  aftermath and rebuilding, 23–27
  health crisis of, 24–25
  legacy of, 28–29
  pre-1906 event, 20–22
Sancho, Luis, 117
Sanitation, 66–68, 110
Santa Barbara oil spill, 159, 161–162
SARS. *See* Severe acute respiratory syndrome (SARS)
Satcher, David, 104
Schleifstein, Mark, 40–42
Schmitz, Eugene, 26
Scientific advancement, 59
Sedgwick, Charles B., 22
Serious Thoughts Occasioned by the Late Earthquake at Lisbon (Wesley), 12
Severe acute respiratory syndrome (SARS), 50, 108–110, 173
  emergence, spread, and cycle of, 111–113
  Hong Kong outbreak, 113–114
  modern era fears, 115–116
  science of, 114–115
Shepard, F. P., 13
Shilts, Randy, 102–103
Shore-lining, 40
Short, James, xix
A Short Discourse Concerning Pestilential Contagion and The Methods to be Used to Prevent It (Meade), 62
Silent Spring (Carson), 94
Simoson, Robert, 37–38
Single Integrated Operational Plan, 128–129
Smallpox, 88–91
  infrastructure for combat, 89–91
Smith, Adam, 60

Snow, John, 68–69, 71–72
Society
  ability to predict/prepare for
    crisis, 6
  church's role in, 6, 55
  enhancing institutional reflexivity,
    174
  humankind's role in, 5
  mutual assistance in, 6
  in plague crisis, 55
  responses to disaster/crisis, 172–173
  risk and harm, 174–175
  understanding disasters/crises,
    175–176
"The Sources of Soviet Conduct"
  (Kennan), 126
Starr, Isaac, 81
Sternberg, George, 92
Stewart, William H., 96–97
Stimson, Henry, 123
Strategic Arms Limitation Interim
  Agreement, 130
Strategic Defense Initiative (SDI), 130
Strauss, Lewis, 133, 174
Straussman, Fritz, 121
Superfund Act, 149
Szilard, Leo, 120–123

T
Technology, science, and crisis, 117.
  risk and, 118
  technological determinism, 118
  See also Nuclear era.
Theodicy (Leibniz), 7
"Theoretical Possibilities and
  Consequences of Major
  Accidents in Large Nuclear
  Power Plants" (WASH 740),
  136–137, 175

Three Mile Island accident, 119,
  139–140, 175
Torrey Canyon spill (1967), 160–161
Toxic waste, 119
Truman Doctrine, 126
Truman, Harry S., 123, 126–127,
  134, 160
Tsunamis, 3
  twentieth century warning
    initiatives, 13–14
  Indian Ocean (2004), 14–17
  Lisbon (1755) disaster, 8–11

U
Union Carbide
  Bhopal accident, 151–154
  Bhopal case/litigation, 154–155
  history in India, 152–153
Union Oil well spill, 161
United Nations Children's Fund
  (UNICEF), 98, 105
United Nations Development
  Program (UNDP), 103, 105
United Nations Educational,
  Scientific and Cultural
  Organization (UNESCO), 105
United Nations Population Fund
  (UNFPA), 105
United States Agency for
  International Development
  (USAID), 90
U.S. Atomic Energy Commission, 133
U.S. Centers for Disease Control, 91
U.S. Department of the Interior,
  160
U.S. Geological Survey, 28
U.S. National Oceanic and
  Atmospheric Administration
  (NOAA), 14

U.S. Public Health Service, 74–75
Urban growth and sanitation, 66–68

V

Vaccination, 48
Vance, Harold, 136
Voltaire, 7–10, 60, 173

W

Wagner, Walter, 117
Water Pollution Control Act, 162
Weather prediction and control, 35
Wells, H. G., 120
Wesley, John, 12, 173
Wilcox, Ansley, II, 145
Wilkins, John, 59
World Bank, 105

World Conference on Disaster
    Reduction (2005), 17
World Health Organization (WHO),
    50, 85, 88–91
    Global Health Intelligence
        Network (GPHIN), 111, 116
    Global Outbreak Alert and
        Response Network (GOARN),
        111, 116
    HIV/AIDS, 94–96, 100, 105
    International Health Regulations,
        110
    SARS outbreak, 108–110
The World Set Free (Wells), 120
Wren, Christopher, 59
Wyman, Walter, 25

Z

Zhdanov, Viktor, 90

About the Author

Kyle Farmbry is Associate Dean of the Graduate School and is an Associate Professor in the School of Public Affairs and Administration (SPAA) at Rutgers University–Newark. Dr. Farmbry has served as a Fulbright New Century Scholar, in which capacity he engaged in research examining factors of youth entrepreneurial and civic engagement in South Africa. In addition to *Crisis, Disaster, and Risk: Institutional Response and Emergence*, he is author of *Administration and the Other: Explorations of Diversity and Marginalization in the Political Administrative State* (2009). Dr. Farmbry received his BA, MPA, and Ph.D. degrees from The George Washington University.

For Product Safety Concerns and Information please contact our EU
representative GPSR@taylorandfrancis.com
Taylor & Francis Verlag GmbH, Kaufingerstraße 24, 80331 München, Germany

www.ingramcontent.com/pod-product-compliance
Ingram Content Group UK Ltd.
Pitfield, Milton Keynes, MK11 3LW, UK
UKHW020941180425
457613UK00019B/496